MEN WHO BATTER:

An Integrated Approach For Stopping Wife Abuse

Edward W. Gondolf
Domestic Violence Study Center
Indiana University of Pennsylvania

Foreword By Maria Roy

LP **Learning Publications, Inc.**
Holmes Beach, Florida

Library of Congress Cataloging in Publication Data

Gondolf, Edward W., 1948-
    Men who batter.

    Bibliography: p.
    Includes index.
    1. Family violence — United States — Prevention.
    2. Wife abuser — Counseling of. 3. Men — United States —
    Psychology. I. Title
    HQ809.3.U5G66   1985   362.8'2   83-83313
    ISBN 0-918452-79-1

Learning Publications, Inc.
5351 Gulf Drive
P.O. Box 1338
Holmes Beach, FL 34218-1338

Printing: 8 7 6 5   Year: 3 2 1 0

Printed in the United States of America.

Acknowledgments

I have been fortunate to meet and work with some of the many individuals striving to end the anguish of wife abuse. Their unremitting toil demonstrated to me that change can be accomplished despite the foreboding odds—and that a book such as this is warranted.

In particular, Diana Brandi, with whom I am married, put in endless hours as a founding board member of Oasis Women's Center in Alton, Illinois, and thus introduced me to the challenges of violence against women. Margarette Bohannon, as director of Oasis, displayed an accommodating spirit without losing her feminist edge, while helping me find my way into the field. Craig Norberg and Don Long of RAVEN, St. Louis, offered me expert training and encouragement in my initial counseling of men who batter. Rich Jenkins, a former batterer, proved to me that men can make substantial changes in themselves and help others to do the same.

Several individuals assisted more directly in the compiling of this book. My colleagues Chuck Flynn and Bob Ackerman prompted me to turn my experience into a guidebook and pointed the way to a publisher. Melanie Diantonis, Jeff Truscott, Linda Gensler, Sharon King, and Romona McCarthy worked as research assistants to collect and review the research reports that underlie Chapter 1 and 2. Three experts in the field offered a careful critique of the manuscript amidst their heavy schedules: Don Long, former staff of RAVEN and presently co-chair of the National Organization for Changing Men; Dave Russell, director of the Second Step

105959

program for men in Pittsburgh; and Linda Rouse, University of Texas—Arlington, a researcher on battering. Sharon Richwine of the Indiana University of Pennsylvania Sociology Department kindly typed and retyped the tedious manuscripts, and Danna Downing as editor refined the writing and moved it toward publication.

In short, a collection of individuals have helped to bring this book into being. I formally thank them all for their contributions to this work. More importantly, their willingness, enthusiasm and support for this project assure me that it is time to reckon decisively with men who are violent.

Foreword

My first reaction to this book is relief. I am relieved to find such a book has been written with its special focus on men who batter.

By reason of an objective analysis of the political issues, some of which are controversial, and a thorough review of the literature, *Men Who Batter* lays the foundation and builds the groundwork for constructing concrete solutions to one of our nation's most horrific and ubiquitous social problems—the senseless, gratuitous violence of men who batter women.

I feel comfort and reassurance in knowing that the book can be a bridge to understanding why some men batter and how professionals and service providers can help them to help themselves.

Of course, helping batterers to help themselves is crucial. Therapeutic resources and professional training are a must. Without them, help does not exist and abusive partners do not have an option for change. I like to think of this book as a declaration of "pro change through the provision of choice." The book is a tool for change. Every batterer who reaches out for help should have the right to change his negative behaviors, should have the right to ask for help and receive it, should have the right to take responsibility for his actions, and should have the right to stop himself from hitting his partner again. *Men Who Batter* insures the batterer these options for responsible change.

This book also analyzes strategies for social action and offers excellent suggestions for facilitating change. In short, *Men Who Batter* presents a well-balanced comprehensive blueprint for diminishing patriarchal sexism and strengthening the emergence of a new gentler identity for men.

Anyone who is interested in helping to deter violence against women should find this book helpful. This book not only describes the ways and means of offering supervised help to batterers who express a desire to stop battering women, but it also addresses the larger issue of sexism in our society.

Maria Roy
AWAIC, Inc.
Editor/Author of
The Abusive Partner
and *Battered Women*

Table Of Contents

viii

Preface

Women's shelter workers, law enforcement officials, and family service counselors have increasingly recommended that more be done with the perpetrators of wife abuse—the men who batter. Consequently, there has been a groundswell of programs to counsel and aid the batterer to stop his violence. Nearly 150 men's programs have emerged in the last five years, but the call for more continues. There is, as a result, mounting demand for training sessions and instructional materials to assist in establishing new programs, adapting existing social services, and expanding the emerging men's programs. This book, as the title suggests, is designed to aid in this development. It is the first effort to consolidate a diverse field into a coherent strategy for helping men who batter.

The movement to develop programs for batterers is yet in its infancy and frought with controversy, as well as great promise. *Men Who Batter* sorts out the prevalent issues and vying options among men's programs in order to guide social service workers toward a viable program of their own. In the midst of extreme philosophical positions, it poses some compromises that may minimize controversy and solidify the gains made by existing programs. The book integrates, in the process, a variety of approaches, research, and field experience to support a model of supervised, self-help men's groups. But the outcome could easily be adapted by therapists, shelter staff, or social workers to meet their needs and resources.

However, the book is not simply a grab bag of techniques and easy exercises to cure the batterer. My experience is that too much attention is given to technique, and too little to the festering issues of format, philosophy, and approach. This book, therefore, discusses the issues, as well as considers appropriate techniques. With this information, new programs can develop an attitude, as well as establish important procedures.

In developing services to help men, there is, nonetheless, one fundamental stipulation: men's services should be closely coordinated with, if not directed by women's services. The ten year struggle to establish women's shelters across the country has moved shelter staff to an important position of expertise and leadership—a position that should be heeded and used as a resource by men's programs.

Furthermore, it is misleading, I believe, to characterize domestic violence as a collaboration between husbands and wives. A wife's behavior may reinforce her husband's violence, but male violence is irrefutably excessive and severe. Even if a wife were to nag, manipulate, or assault her husband, she does not deserve to be beaten or tormented. The man is ultimately responsible for his violent behavior and must be held accountable for it.

Another fundamental assumption underlying this book is that wife abuse is a social problem. It is deeply rooted in social, cultural, economic and political factors that sanction violence and the subjection of women. To treat men psychologically so that they can control their impulses and anger is not sufficient. Men who batter must be helped, therefore, to offset the imposing socialization and institutional supports that predispose them to commit violence against women.

Men who batter act violently toward women as much out of their efforts to maintain control as out of stress. They are generally not mentally ill or maliciously criminal. In fact, the majority of men who batter are not that much different from men who do not batter. Therefore, the batterer's conceptions of masculinity have to be confronted as much as his intrapersonal conflicts. Ultimately, he has to be educated to address pressures in his workplace, local bar, and community—as well as in his home—to act out the traditionally violent and power-hungry male.

With these assumptions, *Men Who Batter* first discusses the issues associated with wife abuse and programs for abusers. Secondly, the book outlines a specific program strategy that addresses format and organization, a counseling curriculum, and an agenda for community action. This presentation will hopefully add momentum, or at least reinforcement, to the movement to stop men from abusing women. Men can and must change.

1

Programs for Men Who Batter

In recent years, incidents of wife beating have been dramatically paraded before the public. Countless newspaper and magazine articles have presented horrifying case studies. Husbands have not only shoved, slapped, punched, and kicked their wives, but have also beaten them into unconsciousness, sadistically raped them, and terrorized them with weapons. Some accounts relate the husband stalking for months the wife who had finally left him and threatening to kill those who did not divulge her whereabouts. Groundbreaking books, like Martin's *Battered Wives* (1976) and Langley and Levy's *Wife Beating: The Silent Crisis* (1977), further substantiated the violence against women, as have more recent assessments of case studies, such as Walker's *The Battered Woman* (1979) and Pagelow's *Woman-Battering* (1981).

Wife Abuse as a Social Problem

There is little doubt that wife beating has become an acute social problem in the United States. A variety of studies confirm that the incidence of abuse is well beyond the exceptional. It is estimated that one in two women will be abused during the course of marriage (Walker, 1979). A national survey found that each year one out of six couples experience at least one violent act; one in eight couples inflicts abuse that causes serious injury, and one in twenty-five marriages is plagued with what amounts to perpetual brutality (Straus, Gelles, and Steinmetz, 1980). Subsequent studies have elaborated the gruesome picture (see Table 1-1).

The litany of statistics suggests that violence in the home dwarfs other categories of violent crime. In fact, 34% of all violent offenses reported to the police in two Scottish cities were assaults between family members. Seventy-six percent of assaults were committed against wives by husbands—only 1% against husbands by wives (Dobash and Dobash, 1979). In sum, violence between spouses is of epidemic proportions. As the most prominent researchers conclude: (Straus, Gelles, and Steinmetz, 1980:50) "If any other crime or risk to physical well-being involved almost two million wives and two million husbands per year, plus much larger numbers at some point in marriage, a national emergency would probably be declared." This observation lends support to the notion that "the marriage license is a hitting license" (Gelles, 1974). There is accompanying evidence that cohabitating couples also experience high levels of violence (Yllo and Straus, 1978).

The abuse of women has been with us for a long time. In ancient Egypt, men were expected to bash their wives teeth out with a brick if they spoke out against them, and the medieval church sanctioned flogging of disobedient wives (Metzger, 1978). As recently as colonial times, a husband was allowed to punish his wife with a stick no bigger than his thumb (Davidson, 1978). Historical accounts of battering (Van Vuuren, 1973; Martin, 1976; Lesse, 1979) inform us not only that wife abuse has long been endorsed as well as tolerated, but also that this legacy is very much with us today despite the dismantling of formal sanctions. As one historian concludes (Metzger, 1978): "Men today batter their wives for the same reasons that men have battered women throughout history: because they have believed it their right, their privilege, and their duty to do so."

If wife abuse has been so much with us, why has it become such a public issue only in recent years? In part, wife abuse has been considered to be a personal matter. Much of contemporary

Table 1-1: Domestic Violence Information

- It is estimated that one-half of all married women are beaten at least once by their husbands. FBI statistics reveal that a woman is beaten every 18 seconds.

- 25% of all victims of domestic violence are pregnant women.

- One in seven women is raped by her husband sometime during their relationship. One in four has an unwanted sexual experience. A Denver study revealed that 34% of the battered women had been raped in their marriage at least once.

- In a study of domestic violence and the police in Kansas City, Missouri, it was found that police had responded to disturbance calls at the address of homicide victims or suspects at least once in the two years before the homicide in 90% of the cases, and five or more times in 50% of the cases.

- Domestic violence is prevalent in every social, economic, racial, educational and religious sector of society. In wealthy Montgomery County, Maryland, police received as many domestic disturbance calls as were received in the same period in Harlem, New York.

- Estimates on the incidence of child abuse range from one million to four million cases each year. Two thousand children die each year from abuse inflicted by a parent or caretaker.

- 80% of all men in American prisons were abused children.

- Every five years, the death toll of persons killed by relatives and acquaintances equals that of the entire Vietnam War.

- Incest researchers conclude that 10-20% of American children are victims of child sexual assault by a parent or parent figure. Ninety percent of the victims are female; 90% of the abusers are fathers or stepfathers.

- An estimated seven million children are beaten by a sibling in a single year.

- In a Massachusetts study of abuse of elderly persons residing in non-institutionalized settings, 86% of the abusers were relatives, 80% of the victims were women and 40% of the abused received visible injuries.

Cited in: Del Martin, *Battered Wives*. New York: Pocket Books, 1977, pp. 14-15.

society believes that "a man's home is his castle." In other words, what goes on behind closed doors is to be overlooked; it is the man's business what he does there. This attitude is reflected in the familiar quip: "You got to knock her around a little to keep her in line."

Social scientists, as well, are guilty of "selective inattention" (Gelles, 1977) and conservatism (Pleck et al., 1978) in investigating the phenomena. Although researchers rummage through all sorts of social pathology, there was virtually no substantial study of wife abuse until the early seventies. In fact, it was not until 1972 that a heading for "spouse abuse" appeared in social science indexes. The five small studies that preceded this period dismissed the problem largely as the result of wife provocation. The abuse, in this way, was relegated to a personal, psychological deficiency and left at that. One study (Snell et al., 1964), for instance, depicted the batterers' wives as frigid, manipulative, and spiteful. Similarly, medical doctors often advised abused women arriving at a hospital to take a sedative in order to calm themselves and make them less likely to antagonize their husbands (see Stark et al., 1979). Moreover, insensitive response from law enforcement agencies led less than two percent of abused women to report battering incidents to the police (Dobash and Dobash, 1979).

The feminist movement has to be credited with establishing wife abuse in our vocabulary (Schechter, 1982). As the movement exposed the under-representation and exploitation of women in American society, violence against women surfaced as a "women's issue." Rape, wife beating, sexual harassment, and pornography all became evidence of the abuse to which women are subjected. These abuses are a means, according to most feminists, to terrorize women. They help keep them in "their place"—that is, make them docile, obedient and subservient. It made sense, then, for women to fight one of the most blatant oppressions of their sex—wife abuse—as part of their cause. The larger political issues were, in fact, brought down to a dramatic personal level with this domestic issue.

There was, also, a variety of concerned factions that began to rally around the "women's issue," but more for practical reasons than ideological ones. Social workers, clergy, family therapists, nurses, alcohol counselors, and even police encountered many women with problems related to abuse. To them, wife abuse became a humanistic issue that demanded a broad response. Interestingly, the "professionals" not only offered their support later in time, but also are still marginally involved in the movement against wife abuse, in comparison to their outright leadership in the work against child abuse. Yet, this is true when there are twice as many women beaten each year as children (Finklehor, 1983; Borkowski et al., 1983).

Wife abuse not only affects the victimized women; society as a whole bears an inordinate penalty for what happens in the home. Countless battered women remain physically or emotionally injured, are unable to support themselves, and must receive welfare, medical, legal and shelter assistance (Pagelow, 1981). Equally as devastating are the consequences borne by the children of the abused. Numerous studies now document the emotional difficulties "yo-yo" children suffer as a result of witnessing abuse, being abused, having to relocate, and living in shelters (NSPCC, 1977; Pfouts et al., 1982). The children's performance in school is understandably poor; they are more prone toward delinquency, and are more likely to grow up to be adult abusers and abused (Owens and Straus, 1975; Cornell and Gelles, 1982). Even the men who batter suffer some consequences. Many fall into deep depression if the wife leaves. Consequently, their performance at work deteriorates. They tend to increase their drinking and often end up in automobile accidents or barroom fights.

Consequently, within ten years time, diligent grassroots coalitions of feminists and social service workers have been able to establish over 500 shelters nationwide, as well as another 500 safe-home networks and women's resource centers. The response has been sustained in part by the national ERA campaign, the National Organization of Women, and the Statewide Coalitions Against Domestic Violence, but also includes anti-abortionists and anti-ERA proponents. The surge of support and service in this short time is, by all standards, astounding.

The movement to address wife abuse, however, appears at this juncture to be adopting a new emphasis—developing treatment for the men who batter. It is becoming increasingly evident that men who batter must be confronted, if the incidence of wife abuse is to be reduced. The movement to establish shelters for battered women has brought a significant reprieve for many of the abused; however, more than 30-50% of the women in shelters return to battering relationships (cited in Martin, 1976:232). Court "orders of protection" are underutilized and difficult to enforce (Quarm and Schwartz, 1983). Even if the abusive relationship is severed, the male frequently finds another mate to abuse (Shainess, 1977). Consequently, a number of researchers on wife abuse (Walker, 1979; Fleming, 1979) strongly advocate counseling services for the men. Some have even recommended more conjoint counseling—that is, the abused and the abuser being counseled together (Gelles, 1982; Weitzman, 1982). This new direction toward servicing the men who batter is, however, being taken with caution, hesitation, and some objection.

Services for the Abuser?

An unavoidable debate surrounds the movement to develop counseling services for batterers. Radical feminists, in particular, pose some challenging questions to the increasing popularity of men's programs. They have suspicion that men's programs may be perpetuating the problem of abuse rather than addressing it. Men's programs have been accused of making batterers feel better about themselves and even blame their victims for provoking the abuse. Some counseling services and self-help groups ease the batterer's feelings of guilt and help him restrain his violence, rather than root out the sexist attitudes behind the violence. Moreover, the preoccupation with counseling fails to motivate men to make changes in the social institutions which reinforce their violent behavior. As one radical feminist who has labored long in the shelter movement advocates:

> Men face the task of working through their networks with other men to declare unacceptable the unequal power dynamics between men and women, challenge institutions, and reshape public consciousness as they refuse the privileges available to them. In the long run, men and women together must work to define and live egalitarian sexual and social relationships in the context of a struggle to end exploitation and oppression (Schechter, 1982:240).

Feminists are also concerned about the increasing competition for funds. Many women's shelters, while struggling to keep their doors open, have sorely inadequate facilities. In New York City, for instance, as many as 85% of the callers to shelters are turned away (cited in Schechter, 1982:12), and in many rural areas there continues to be no service at all. Most shelters, furthermore, lack child care programs for the two-thirds of their visitors who are children and have insufficient staff to maintain community education and training.

In sum, feminists believe that women and children should be cared for first (see Morrison, 1982; McLaughlin, 1982) and that if men want to work on stopping domestic violence, they should raise funds for the shelters. After all, men in our society generally have better access to monetary resources than women. Moreover, the men's organizations or programs should be careful that they are not competing for power, as well as for funds. The women in the shelter movement often perceive the emerging men's services as a means of usurping their leadership and negating their anger.

Many shelter workers wonder whether men deserve any sort of consolation considering the daily picture of brutality inflicted by men—bloodied faces, bruised flesh, broken arms, injured genitals of women and children. In this light, they feel it may be more appropriate for men who batter to be put in jail and severely punished as they would for an equivalent assault against a stranger, rather than coddled by some counseling service (see Armstrong, 1983). The "criminalization" of abusers may ultimately be warranted but in itself may not be sufficient. There remains, as many shelter workers observe, a reluctance on the part of many battered women to prosecute the battering men, and an increased hostility in the few men who are jailed for their assault and eventually released.

The debate over abuser programs reflects the persistent dichotomy between social service and social action proponents (see Dobash and Dobash, 1981). As suggested, the rift between these two orientations is particularly pronounced in the domestic violence field because of the prominent role of the women's movement in the "discovery" of wife abuse and the negligent response of many doctors, police, mental health workers, and clergy. Those entering the field, therefore, must eventually reckon with the strong differences in orientation and develop a stance of their own. If the question of orientation is not decisively addressed, their organization is more likely to fall into internal controversy over philosophical differences, or draw external disrespect for its ambiguous positioning.

Underlying the controversy are some fundamentally different assumptions about wife abuse and how to address it (see Table 1-2). The social service proponents—conventional mental health workers, psychotherapists, social workers, and clergy—more generally analyze wife abuse as the manifestation of aggressive communication patterns sustained by both husband and wife. The male may inflict the greater harm, but both male and female, in a sense, contribute to abuse when they repeat behaviors which they more than likely learned from their abusive parents.

The social action proponents, on the other hand, identify the spouse abuse as "women beating" in order to emphasize that the violence is inordinately committed by men against women—or by women against men in self defense. Women, according to this position, bear the brunt of unequal power relations in which men exercise their dominance through the use of violent force. Abused

Table 1-2: Social Service Versus Social Action Approaches To Wife Abuse

	Social Service	Social Action
Issue:	Spouse abuse Victimization Both husband and wife suffer	Women battering Oppression Violence is against women
Cause:	Family interaction patterns Learn violence from parents Men suffer poor impulse control Victim provocation Violent culture reinforced by competitive economy	Unequal power relationships Learn place in male dominated society Men assert desired control History of male dominance Sexism institutionalized in patriarchal society
Response:	Humanist social services Counseling and assertiveness training Institutionalized treatment Professionalization	Feminist social action Empowerment and politicizing Grassroots community organizing Self-help programs

wives, as a consequence, are forced to live in terror amidst un-predictable and unwarranted explosions of battering.

Accordingly, there are different responses to wife abuse. The social service proponents, regarding domestic violence more as a humanist issue, consider both women and men to be suffering from violent relationships. Social service proponents maintain that ultimately, both the abused and abuser deserve counseling assistance. Both need to be taught assertive communication that enables them to express their needs and feelings without lapsing into violence or provocation. Ideally, social services that treat the violent partners should be institutionalized and become more professional.

The radical feminists obviously feel women need and deserve to be helped, but their goal is not simply to make the battered wives better communicators or independent from their batterers. Rather, they feel that women need to be empowered. That is, they need to develop a political sense which recognizes the relation of their abuse to the structure of society and fosters confidence to challenge and change that structure. Exploitive advertising, pornography, and wage differences, for instance, contribute to the degradation of women and make them vulnerable targets of male violence. Therefore, oppression in general must be readdressed at the grassroots level, where women can join together to take charge of their own lives.

Professionals are likely to establish a hierarchy in which the experts speak for the victims and perpetuate dependency. In fact, doctors, psychologists, and criminal justice officials have more often tolerated domestic violence instead of attacking it. Further-more, the formal funding necessary to maintain a professional staff can force an innovative organization to compromise with the in-stitutions it seeks to change. Therefore, self-help services motivated toward social action are the answer, according to the feminist view.

The dichotomy between humanists and radical feminists, however instructive, may be an artificial one. In actuality, neither social service workers or radical feminists hold monolithic theoretical postures. There are social service proponents who emphasize a psychoanalytic as opposed to social learning analysis. I have been a client of one "feminist therapist" who practiced transactional therapy and another who employed a gestalt approach. Among social action advocates, there are those who sympathize with Betty Friedan's assertions in *The Second Stage* (1981) supporting the woman's domestic role and relationship with men. On the other hand, there are those activist feminists who endorse the socialist leanings of Angela Davis registered in *Women, Race and Class* (1981).

Most field workers concede that both social service and social action must ultimately be accomplished, and that both a violent culture and a patriarchal society must be addressed. The challenge is that treating the immediate suffering of wife abuse can divert energy from changing the society which sustains the social problem. On the other hand, the ideological preoccupations of a social change movement can mute one's compassion and sensitivity to the victims and perpetrators in need of help.

If developed properly, social services can serve as an arena where social action principles are taught and refined, as well as where hurting individuals are helped. After all, broad social issues essentially do affect the individual and can be addressed in personal ways. Social services can ease the suffering and awaken potential. For instance, women who are free from a sense of subjection and men who are alert to the misuse of privilege are more likely to act in a constructive rather than destructive manner, thereby making a contribution to society at large.

This is not to minimize the debate over men's services but to suggest that a mediation of the conflicting points of view is plausible. Abusive men need to change, regardless of one's perspective. They need to stop their violent behavior and start sharing power. Where better to start such a change process than within the men's programs?

Professionalized men's programs can be maintained without undermining the drive toward substantial change, if established with some stipulations. If the men's programs are closely coordinated with shelters, competition for funds and leadership can be minimized. In some communities, the presence of men's programs adjunct to the shelters has actually increased support of the shelter. Some factions of the community felt more inclined to donate because they felt that the men's program added to the effectiveness of the shelter.

As for the format of these services, most shelters and existing men's programs necessarily rely on a combination of experienced staff and volunteers. On one hand, some professionalism seems warranted to interpret complex personal problems associated with wife abuse and to organize the community for financial support and political leverage. Without some professionalism, worthwhile movement efforts often become disorganized and undermined by personal infighting.

Yet, the most successful programs in changing behavior are those with movement ties. They tend to be more responsive to the needs of those whom they serve and also present an uncompromised commitment that has an impact. Their dedication to the ideal that people are able to, and deserve to be better, is contagious. Such commitment is difficult to sustain, as high turnover rates indicate, but without staff dedication as well as caring, programs can easily become custodial instead of oriented toward change.

In sum, integration of social service and social action is warranted. Observers of alternative social services (Holleb and Abrams, 1975), in fact, note a stage development from grassroots self-help to professional organizations, which can culminate in a combination of social service and social action features (see Table 1-3). In the first stage of "consensual anarchy," innovative programs begin with ideological fervor and a fluid structure, but often without practical planning and consistent services. As the organization encounters an increased demand for its services and internal power conflicts, it assumes a stage of "differentiation" to stabilize its operations. There appears a more delineated hierarchy and a de-emphasis of ideology. At this juncture, the organization might

Table 1-3: The Organization Life Cycle

Stage:	Consensual Anarchy	Differentiation (Informal, Formal, Bureaucratic)	Consensual Democracy
Orientation:	Social Movement-Ideological	Social Services-Professional	Alternative Services-Communalism and competence
Characteristics:	Fluid membership Undifferentiated tasks Highly ideological Crisis orientation High energy	Administrative hierarchy Specialized staffing Foundation or public funding Elaborate planning Greater efficiency and stability	Return to consensual forms Clear rules and procedures Defined boundaries and entrance requirements Structures to share work and feelings
Leadership:	Charismatic leaders Consensual decision making No formal procedures	Formal decision making procedures Administrators supervise operations Highly trained or professional	Informal and shared authority Independent components or subgroups Total staff decides major decisions
Staff rewards:	Commitment to ideals Social contact Personal growth Individual autonomy	Job security Competitive salary Recognition from other professionals	Involvement in planning A sense of community Increasing effectiveness
Problems and Pressures:	Sparse funds Unclear procedures Power struggles Inconsistent services Sloppy public relations High staff turnover	Decrease in autonomy and innovation Loss of personal commitment Absence of ideology and vision Competition with other services Breakdown of personal communications Impersonal response to clients	Low salaries Slow decision making Loss of clinical time Funding difficult to obtain Limited referrals Narrow scope of services

Adapted from: Gordon Holleb and Walter Abrams, *Alternatives in Community Mental Health*. Boston: Beacon, 1975.

adopt a phase of "informal differentiation" in which a family sense remains. Or, it may move to "formal differentiation" in which the organizational decision-making procedures and division of labor are further defined and regulated. As policy becomes more refined and funding more extensive, the organization may become a "bureaucracy" which is stable and consistent, but not innovative. In this phase of differentiation, the intense commitment and ideology that initiated the organization are lost to a specialized administration. However, there is lower staff turnover, organizational recognition, and competitive salaries.

A social service organization, however, can achieve a stage beyond these phases of differentiation. In "consensual democracy," the organization maintains procedures for decision-making and structures for sharing work; but generally its salaries are lower, obtaining funds is more difficult, and the scope of referrals is limited. Nonetheless, an organization with consensual democracy can become an influential agent for social change, especially when it is linked with other "collective" organizations. This model is obviously more in line with feminist conceptions of organizational structure and yet assures dependable services that are accessible and responsive. Professional pressures and difficulty in obtaining financial support, however, often make this stage difficult to attain and maintain, even though it may represent the ideal mix of service and social action.

A Typology of Programs for Men Who Batter

Since 1977, a variety of programs designed to deal directly with the batterer have emerged (see Watts and Courtois, 1981; Roberts, 1982; Mettger, 1982). Leading the way are a number of self-help groups established in response to the women's liberation movement and the accompanying men's liberation movement. EMERGE in Boston and RAVEN in St. Louis are the two most prominent of these groups, with reputable self-help group counseling (Adams and McCormick, 1982). Second, an increasing number of women's shelters have started adjunct programs for the abusers (Garnet and Moss, 1982). Third, some mental health and family services offer psychotherapy for batterers (Geller, 1982; Weitzman and Dreem, 1982; Holmes,1981). (See Table 1-4 for summary.)

In 1980 *Response*, a newsletter of the Center for Women Policy Studies, listed 80 counseling programs for men who batter. A more recent overview of men's programs in the December 1982 *Response* estimated that 150 batterer programs now exist. The figures appear to confirm an emerging trend in the treatment of domestic violence. The course of this trend toward men's programs, however, is much less certain, because such a diversity of approaches and formats persists (see Roberts, 1982).

Obviously there are advantages and disadvantages to each approach that must be weighed. Each of the prevailing approaches is, therefore, reviewed to help prospective program staff chart out the field and choose the route most suitable for them. For reasons that will be discussed, this book considers the supervised self-help groups to be the most effective format for dealing with batterers. Other program formats, however, do have contributions to make and can adapt the integrated approach outlined here.

Mental Health Programs

The conventional mental health programs employ primarily psychotherapy, stress management, anger control, and conflict resolution techniques in an effort to bring impulse, stress, and anger under control. These programs seem particularly adept at ferreting out the internal psychological conflicts that give rise to abusive behavior. Considering the aggressive behavior socialized into men and the stressful competition of many men's occupations, this approach may have some merit. Many family counselors, furthermore, recommend conjoint counseling with the abused and abuser, since, from their point of view, the abuse is an outgrowth of a weak family system. Just stopping the violence is not sufficient and may not be attained, until there is a change in the interpersonal

Table 1-4: A Typology of Men's Services

Service:	Mental Health Programs	Shelter Adjunct Program	Self-Help Organizations
Features:	Concern with impulse control and stress Individual psychotherapy and couples counseling Professional referrals Treatment of related problems: alcoholism, nutrition, mental illness	Group counseling Coordination of men and women services Leadership and supervision by women shelter staff Expertise in domestic violence	Peer counseling and self-help format Free of social service stigma Relative autonomy Anti-sexist education
Innovations:	Court-ordered counseling programs	Community intervention systems	Organization of men for social action
Shortcomings:	Male resistance Fear of stigma Maintain isolation Institutionalized violence and sexism not addressed	Women's safety and privacy possibly jeopardized Abusive men resent shelters	Limited funding Reinforces male separatism and without professional guidance encourage sexist attitudes Lack of professional psychological assessment

relations of the husband and wife, and the unspoken "rules" that structure their relationship.

Both individual and couples counseling may be combined within this mental health approach. The partners might be counseled first individually then jointly or in any combination of individual and couples counseling. The individual counseling along with the couples counseling allows for the separate partners to reconsider the dynamics of the joint session, as well as reckon with their personal shortcomings. Some mental health programs are also beginning to form groups of batterers and battered that rely on group counseling to support those in an abusive relationship. Generally, the emphasis in these groups is still on helping the individuals gain greater psychological insight into their mutual problem.

Some mental health programs have, furthermore, begun to establish programs for the court-ordered counseling of men who batter (Ganley, 1981; Dreas et al., 1982). These programs, directed by professionally trained counselors, are designed to give batterers an understanding of their abuse and some fundamental techniques to control it. Some in the field have suggested that the court-ordered counseling may be the best approach, since such a small portion of the batterers presently volunteer for counseling programs. However, intense resistance from court-ordered clients often undermine the therapeutic aspects of counseling. Consequently, some court-ordered programs have instituted required classes like those for drunken drivers (see Frank and Houghton, 1982). The court-referred clients are "educated," rather than treated, with a variety of films, speakers, readings, lectures, and class exercises which confront them with the responsibility for and consequences of their behavior. Ideally, the program will prompt the clients to reconsider their behavior and willingly submit to a therapeutic counseling program.

The scope of these mental health programs is, of course, limited and may need broadening. A small portion of batterers, perhaps as many as 15%, are significantly disturbed and do need intense psychotherapy. However, the vast majority of men who batter are not psychologically disturbed in the conventional sense. As previously discussed, their abuse is related to cultural, social, and political practices. Therefore, men who batter must ultimately be educated and organized to offset the social pressures that would lead them back to the battering or perpetuate battering by other men (see Nichols, 1976).

Moreover, most men who batter, and perhaps men in general, are resistant to psychotherapy (Scher, 1981). The abusers with whom I worked were quick to point out that they were "not sick." As one typically noted "I'm no sicky! I don't want any of that psychology stuff. Anyhow, that Sigmund Freud was a perverted alcoholic!" However unfounded the resistance, the men who call for help tremendously fear a loss of control and dependency on someone else. Some researchers hypothesize that the violence is a man's desperate attempt to maintain control when he feels like he is losing it (Gondolf, in press). Counseling is, therefore, perceived as a threat since it represents relinquishing some of one's already threatened control to the counselor. Psychological help, in this way, stigmatizes the batterer as not being manly, but as being weak and deficient.

This is not to say that mental health and family services cannot be adapted to help men who batter, but that their conventional format is not especially suited to this particular clientele. It may be that those specializing in domestic violence and employing a self-help group format are in a better position to "treat" those involved in abuse.

Adjunct Shelter Programs

Serving batterers through the existing shelters, the second approach, may have an advantageous position in this regard. Shelter workers have already developed an expertise on wife abuse and have direct access to the victims of abuse. They can, therefore, assure enough members for group counseling—something that the dispersed counseling services cannot always do. A support group of some kind is essential in treating batterers or the battered; the sharing among group members counters the stigma and isolation often felt in individual or couples counseling.

Since such a large number of abused women eventually return to their abusive partners, many shelter staff feel that it is essential to work with the abuser whenever possible. As mentioned, shelters; like the House of Ruth in Baltimore, Maryland; the Domestic Violence Project in Ann Arbor, Michigan; and AWAIC in New York City; have consequently established their own programs to assist batterers. (Some women's programs collaborate with affiliated men's programs, as does AWARE in Juneau, Alaska, with MEN and AWARE in Denver, Colorado, with AMEND.) Often the adjunct batterer groups meet at a facility separate from the shelter, but usually with a male or female shelter staff member.

An obvious advantage of these programs is that the shelter staff can monitor both sides of the abusive relationship. The staff observing both partners is able to better assure the wife's safety, verify accounts, and bring the couple together when appropriate. Some shelters also have found that this dual approach gives them more legitimacy in the community. Reactionary factions have accused shelters of being havens for separatist feminists who are trying to break up the family. Having men's programs under the auspices of the shelter appeases such opposition, while enabling women to supervise the men's programs and thus assure cooperative funding and compatible philosophies.

This adjunct format has led to some notable innovations, as well. Some shelters have collaborated with a variety of services to develop community intervention systems. The Domestic Abuse Project in Minneapolis, Minnesota, and the Domestic Abuse Intervention Project in Duluth, Minnesota, have established a coordinated effort of professionals, shelter workers, and police to respond to domestic violence (see Star 1983: 148-175). The system delivers services to the men, but also offers special training to mental health counselors, law enforcement officials, and shelter volunteers. In sum, these programs work directly with the community services to coordinate their response to family violence.

There are, of course, some drawbacks to the adjunct programs for men who batter. Battered women are often resentful or fearful about a shelter's association with their abusive partners. Many fear for their safety and want to be rid of their abusers. Even if the men's programs are separate from the shelter, some of the woman's private thoughts might be passed inadvertently through the staff to her husband, since a batterer may attempt to manipulate the staff into divulging his wife's whereabouts and her feelings toward their separation.

The men, on the other hand, are similarly resentful about being associated with shelters. They often perceive them as "hideouts" for their wives, forwarding man-hating ideas. This attitude, of course, is more a reflection of the men's own rigid and prejudiced outlook. Therefore, while it is advantageous to coordinate services for men and women, the men's programs benefit from some separation from the women's shelters and some distinction of their own.

Supervised Self-Help Programs

The third category of men's programs are the organizations independent from shelters, even though they may cooperate with shelter staff. These programs build primarily on self-help dynamics or peer counseling. The men, in a sense, are charged with taking responsibility for changing their own behavior. In the process, they are provided with alternative means to cope with stress or pressure, as well as with support and encouragement from other men undergoing a change in their self-image. There are a number of organizations that share this approach but with differing emphasis. These include Batterers Anonymous chapters dedicated to anger control and anti-sexist collectives like RAVEN and EMERGE concerned more with challenging men's control of women. (See Interrante, 1981, for more on this distinction.)

Branch chapters of Batterers Anonymous have been formed in a number of cities around the country. Founded on many of the principles of Alcoholics Anonymous, Batterers Anonymous gets batterers to work together to stop their abuse. A group of batterers meeting weekly is inexpensive to organize and maintain, especially since the group leader is often a former batterer himself working as a volunteer. Most importantly, in the process of batterers helping themselves, there emerges a sense of self-control, independence, and autonomy compatible with many men's sense of masculinity. The men in the group do not get off easy, however; former batterers are often extremely effective at recognizing and confronting the withdrawal or deceit of other men who batter.

Although the Batterers Anonymous program, in general, appears to be helpful, there are some programs employing the self-help approach that have drawn criticism. Shelter staff, in particular, are often reluctant to work with independent batterer groups. They are concerned that these groups may allow violent men to reinforce each other rather than challenge one another to substantially change. Some shelter workers suggest, therefore, that more professional supervision for men's groups is required. A paid staff member, trained in intervention and confrontation, may be necessary to assure some consistency in the program and proper coordination with shelter programs.

Supervised self-help groups have grown out of the men's movement as a response to violence against women. These programs like RAVEN in St. Louis are based on grassroots efforts of men helping other men to change and respond to issues raised by feminists. These organizations also use a peer counseling approach but with more structure and supervision than the Batterers Anonymous program affords. Generally, these programs are comprised of a nucleus of experienced staff and trained volunteers who guide groups of batterers through eight to sixteen weeks of discussion and exercises. The expert staff are more likely to discern security issues around abuse and personal problems that may warrant intense psychotherapy, medical assistance, or detoxification, than untrained or inexperienced reformed batterers. These programs, also, are better equipped than self control self-help groups to present anti-sexist education to batterers—that is, help the batterers to redefine their roles as men and begin to regard women more as equals.

A few of the anti-sexist programs have begun to move beyond the counseling format. EMERGE, in particular, considers itself a "collective" of men working to end violence against women. Although there are trained counselors and social workers sustaining the organization, the group attempts to maintain a lateral decision making process, rather than a professional hierarchical one. The organization, in this way, is more than a social service. It presents a cooperative model of a male workplace for clients as well as other social services.

EMERGE, in fact, considers itself to be part of a movement organizing men to challenge the sexism in society which induces violence against women. As at RAVEN, participants in the EMERGE program can not only attend group discussion and counseling sessions, but also business meetings, potluck suppers, training sessions, and conferences. This sort of involvement helps men to develop a sense of identity with other men working for broader social change—change that affects other social services, the criminal justice system, and the workplace, as well as the family and community.

2

Research on Wife Abuse

The explanations for wife abuse are as diverse and underdeveloped as the programs to reckon with it. As mentioned in the previous chapter, substantive studies of the acute problem have only emerged in the last ten years. The recent influx of research on abused women has managed to debunk many of the prevailing myths (see Table 2-1), but most of this research has been confined to interviews and case studies of battered women residing in crisis shelters or surveys of former shelter residents (Martin, 1976; Langley and Levy, 1977; Davidson, 1978; Fleming, 1979; Walker, 1979; Pagelow, 1981; Roy, 1977, 1982a; Giles-Sims, 1983).

Regional and national surveys of the general population have confirmed the scope and nature of abuse (Gelles, 1974; Gayford, 1975; Flynn, 1977; Dobash and Dobash, 1979; Straus et al., 1980; Stacey and Shupe, 1983). Many researchers have also attempted to demonstrate that the violence is a complex matter with a variety of psychological and sociological factors at play (Tidmarch, 1976; Straus, 1977, 1980; Goodstein and Page, 1981; Carlson, 1977; Prescott, 1975; Straus et al., 1980; Bern, 1982). Such efforts to come up with conclusive predictors for wife abuse, however, have been sharply criticized as inadequate and misleading. In fact we must be leary of a "whoozle effect"—that is, assuming some marginally substantiated notions are fact (Schumm, et al., 1982).

Table 2-1: Battering Myths and Realities

There are many myths and misunderstandings that surround the phenomenon of wife abuse and help to perpetuate it. The prevailing myths about battering are listed below. They are followed by some of the countering evidence that points toward a more accurate representation of the abuse problem.

* **The Battered Woman Syndrome Affects Only A Small Percentage Of The Population.**

   Nearly two million women a year are abused and nearly 50% of all women are battered sometime during marriage.

* **Battered Women Are Generally Masochistic Or Hysterical.**

   Most abuse is, interestingly, not preceded by provocation.

* **Middle-Class Women Do Not Get Battered As Frequently Or As Violently As Do Poorer Women.**

   Battering appears to cut across classes although it is reported less often in upper classes.

* **Minority-Group Woman Are Battered More Frequently Than Anglos.**

   Different kinds of battering may typify some minority groups, but there is little difference in extent.

* **Religious Beliefs Will Prevent Battering.**

   Staunchly religious men are equally involved in battering.

* **Battered Women Are Uneducated And Have Few Job Skills.**

   The more educated women may be at greater risk.

* **Batterers Are Violent In All Their Relationships.**

   The "Dr. Jekyll and Mr. Hyde" syndrome appears in men who batter, even though it is true that violent men, in general, tend to be abusers.

* **Batterers Are Unsuccessful And Lack Resources To Cope With The World.**

   Batterers, like battered women, come from *all* classes.

* **Drinking Causes Battering Behavior.**

   Alcoholic drinks may reinforce the abuse but are not its cause and should not be used to excuse it.

* **Batterers Are Psychopathic Personalities.**
  The vast majority of batterers are more like men in the general population.

* **Police Can Protect The Battered Woman.**
  Police protection is at best limited and often antagonizes the batterer.

* **The Batterer Is Not A Loving Partner.**
  Batterers, according to the cycle of violence, are often apologetic and affectionate after abuse.

* **A Wife Batterer Also Beats His Children.**
  Batterers more frequently abuse just their wives, although there is often "spillover."

* **Once A Battered Woman, Always A Battered Woman.**
  Women can and do break the cycle—most often through leaving the man who batters.

* **Once A Batterer, Always A Batterer.**
  Men can eventually change with willingness and help.

* **Long-Standing Battering Relationships Can Change For The Better.**
  Without outside intervention, battering tends to repeat itself unless the cycle is decisively interrupted.

* **Battered Women Deserve To Get Beaten.**
  No justification for male violence exists—it is a criminal act.

* **Battered Women Can Always Leave Home.**
  Economic and emotional dependency on the man, responsibility for the children, and threats from the man make it difficult to leave or tempting to return.

* **Batterers Will Cease Their Violence "When We Get Married."**
  Abuse generally increases.

* **Children Need Their Father Even If He Is Violent—Or, "I'm Only Staying For The Sake Of The Children."**
  The exposure to violence is likely to emotionally impair the children.

Adapted from: Lenore Walker, *The Battered Woman*. New York: Harper, 1979, pp. 19-31.

This chapter examines the principal research in the field of wife abuse and its theoretical implications. In the process, a batterer appears to be elusive in that he tends to evade study and treatment. The observations that do prevail suggest, however, that men who batter are violent in response to gender socialization, rather than because they are "insane" or "deviant."

The review of the research first focuses on the efforts to characterize the batterer and then considers the prominent theories used to interpret that characterization. It also reviews the intense debate within these efforts to explain male violence, particularly among those who trace the wife abuse to a violent culture and those who cite the patriarchal society as central. Lastly, the men's liberation literature, which focuses on the debilitating socialization of men in general, is discussed as a means of unifying and redirecting the attempt to understand and help men who batter. Suggested throughout is that men are predisposed to respond inappropriately to their female partners—and this tendency is sustained if not fostered by society itself.

Studies of Wife Abuse

There is little conclusive research on men who batter. The few direct studies of batterers are of small samples (25-50) of highly specialized populations—psychiatric patients (Watson et al., 1982); convicted assaulters (Faulk, 1974); military personnel (Raiha, 1982); alcoholics (Flanzer, 1982); counseling clients (Coleman, 1980). This has led Maria Roy (1982:33), speaking for a number of activists and researchers, to assert that "studies of abusive partners are practically non-existent to date, though the need to understand the problem of violent partnership as a whole is great."

This conspicuous lack of research is due in part to the fact that men typically avoid counselors, the police and even their friends. The few family studies that have attempted to include batterers have noted them to be uncooperative (Gelles, 1974; Levine, 1975). Batterers, in sum, are elusive subjects to study or treat systematically (Star, 1980; Scher, 1981). The lack of research may also be related to the posture of researchers themselves. Male researchers have noticeably neglected to assail this difficult field (Martin, 1976; Fleming, 1979), and the few who have studied abuse made their reputations focusing on battered women rather than battering men.

The prevailing assessments of abusive men, consequently, are derived indirectly from case studies of abused women (Pagelow, 1981; Fleming, 1979; Walker, 1979; and Martin, 1976). This research literature offers a decisive portrait of men who batter, albeit through the eyes of abused women (see Table 2-2). The male batterer is characterized as a debilitated individual of low self-esteem, rigid stereotypes and poor impulse-control. The men typically have a lack of communications skills, faith in traditional sex roles, a marked history of violence, and often abuse alcohol (Powers and Kutash, 1982). (See also Fitch and Pupantonio, 1983.) The majority of batterers, moreover, admit a chronic dissatisfaction with their marriages, retaliation to perceived provocation, and tremendous jealousy of their wives (Coleman, 1980). They seldom, however, have substantial police or psychiatric records (Roy, 1982a).

Three Theoretical Explanations

Three different theoretical positions are generally acknowledged to explain this outward character: psychoanalytic, social learning, and sociopolitical theories (Gelles, 1983; Bagarozzi and Giddings, 1983). The psychoanalytic theories focus on stress, anxiety and anger instilled during child rearing. The social learning theories consider the abuse to be an outgrowth of learned patterns of aggressive communication to which both husband and wife contribute. The sociopolitical theories hold the patriarchal power plays of men oppressing women to be at the heart of wife abuse.

First, *the psychoanalytic theories* frequently depict the abused women as masochistic (Klechner, 1978) or exhibiting "learned helplessness" (Walker, 1979), and the man frought with infantile

Table 2-2: The Abuser's Profile

Wife-batterers can be found in every age group and socioeconomic level: "You wouldn't be able to pick one out on the street," says David Adams of EMERGE, a batterer's program in Boston, Massachusetts. But counselors say that abusive men generally share certain personality traits that contribute to their violent behavior including:

- Low self-esteem resulting from physical or sexual abuse, disapproval or neglect by an alcoholic or authoritarian parent.

- Extreme insecurity and inability to trust others. Batterers have difficulty establishing close friendships and tend to be particularly critical or jealous of their spouses.

- A "need to control" relationships, which stems from a rigidly traditional view of sex roles and parenting.

- A "Jekyll-and-Hyde" type of personality. Very few batterers have previous criminal records or display generally violent behavior. In fact, they can be extremely passive in the face of conflict and bottle up their emotions until they explode in anger.

- Related drug or alcohol problems, sometimes used as an excuse for "losing control" when "provoked" by the spouse.

- A tendency to see themselves as locked in a struggle for survival in a "dog-eat-dog" world.

- An inability to nurture others or express need; a fear of intimacy and being "vulnerable."

- Strong feelings of guilt and failure: "No matter what I do it is not enough."

- Denial of responsibility for their behavior, especially the violence.

From: Alan Predergast, "Facing Up To Being A Wife-Beater," *USA Today*, Wed., August 17, 1983, p. 3D.

hostility and womb envy which he transfers to his wife. Some of the early studies (Snell et al., 1964) explicitly stated that the women brought the battering on themselves. The battered women were supposedly more likely than unbattered women to be frigid, aggressive, and manipulative, in part because of unresolved hostility toward their father. More recent studies suggest that battered women tolerate (Shainess, 1979) or seek out abuse (Lion, 1977; Garbarino and Gilliam, 1980) because of demeaning experiences and socialization that has made them feel guilty and unworthy of anything better.

The men who batter, from this perspective, are fearful and hateful toward women because of the childrearing they have received. Psychoanalysts suggest that by beating a woman, a man is actually rechanneling his resentment for overmothering toward his wife. Schultz (1960) maintains in his research on men who tried to kill their wives that "abusive men transfer their dependency needs from their mothers to their wives and then lash out when their wives cannot or will not meet these needs" (cited in Stacy and Shupe, 1983:91).

Similarly, many female psychoanalysts have observed that men develop hypermasculinity to overcompensate for their emotional insecurities. Men in our society, raised largely by their mothers (Dinnerstein, 1976; Chodorow, 1978; Lesse, 1979) and female school teachers (Sexton, 1973), overexaggerate their masculinity to confirm their male gender against the feminity around them. According to Chodorow (1978:160-167), male development, therefore, entails a "more emphatic individuation and a more defensive firming of experienced ego boundaries." For boys, but not girls, "issues of differentiation have become intertwined with sexual issues." (These theorists consequently urge more male fathering to help antidote the hypermasculinity.)

Those of the psychoanalytical point of view have also indicated that the male resentment toward the mother figure may extend to all women in misogyny. The excessively rational and analytical male is left envious and even intimidated by the female's creative, intuitive and spiritual capacities (Horney, 1932). Women, also, have a biological closeness to nature that men can never duplicate. Most men, in an effort to contain and control what they do not have and cannot understand, have become "woman haters" not only abusing women, but also destroying whatever is of feminine quality including nature herself—that is, the natural environment (Griffin, 1979).

Second, *the social learning theory* characterizes the family as "a cradle of violence" (Straus et al., 1980) where violent behavior is intergenerational (Owens and Straus, 1975; Gelles, 1976; NSPCC, 1977; Carlson, 1977; Pfouts et al., 1981; Pagelow, 1981; Cornell and Gelles, 1982). That is, the batterer learns to be violent as a child by watching or experiencing the violence of his parents, and the battered child similarly learns to be a recipient of violence. As many as 80% of abusers and 30% of the abused wives have witnessed or received abuse as a child (Roy, 1982a; Straus et al., 1980). This sort of evidence leads Straus, Gelles and Steinmetz (1980:121) to conclude: "Over and over again, the statistics suggest the same conclusion. Each generation learns to be violent by being a participant in a violent family." (Dobash and Dobash, 1979, and Rosenbaum and O'Leary, 1982, however, strongly object to using this evidence as the basis of causal inference. The low percentage of women who witnessed violence suggests, if anything, that the batterers learn violence, and the women are not accomplices but more helpless victims.)

The man and the woman become, in this analysis, co-conspirators in a violent relationship. That is, the husband and wife together develop a pattern of attack and counterattack in their communication that leads to violence. As Gelles (1977:57) affirms in his study: "Victims of marital violence (whether they were men or women) were not simply 'whipping boys' or hostility sponges for violent partners. Rather, the victim tended to play an active role in his or her own victimization." In fact the women may be violent in frequency and kind as much as the men, according to Steinmetz' research (1977). Although the incidence in violent acts may be comparable, the men, however, are usually in a position to cause more physical damage because of their strength and stature and their training in violent behavior.

Physical abuse by the man is shown to be sparked by escalating verbal and physical aggression between partners (Straus, 1974; Steinmetz, 1977). Unfair criticisms, rejections of sexual overtures, oversights of expected errands, and disputes over the budget "provoke" acts of aggression. As Straus, Gelles, and Steinmetz (1980: 173) deduce from their research: "It is clear that the more conflicts a couple has, the more likely they are to get into a physical fight. In fact, a persisting severe conflict or something crucial, such as a disagreement over children, is almost sure to end in at least some violence." The aggression between partners mounts, until name-calling turns to push and push to hit. Interestingly, this interpretation that "violence begets violence" tends to counter the ventilation theory often forwarded by psychologists who would have family members "let it all out" short of violence.

Third, *the sociopolitical critique* interprets wife abuse as a manifestation of patriarchy. Our patriarchal or "male dominated" society structurally excludes women from political, business, legal, and religious leadership (see Table 2-3). Women are forced into subordinate roles through two processes: one, discrimination that blocks them from obtaining influential positions in the work force and, secondly, an ideology of inferiority that justifies their lack of opportunity with notions of their innate inferiority. Many women consequently adopt a false consciousness in which they believe it is "right" for them to be subordinate (Dobash and Dobash, 1979:44). Men typically extend their power and privilege to the family as they have throughout history (Davidson, 1978; Lesse, 1979).

The issue of wife abuse, therefore, is not one merely of violence but of power relationships. The man applies the same dictates of control, domination, and authority in the home as he does in society at large. Goode (1971), in his exchange theory analysis of force in the family, notes that the batterer uses force

Table 2-3: The Nature Of The Patriarchy And Its Maintenance

The patriarchy is comprised of two elements: its structure and its ideology. The structural aspect of the patriarchy is manifest in the hierarchical organization of social institutions and social relations. The patriarchy is an organizational pattern that by definitions relegates selected individuals, groups, or classes to positions of power, privilege, and leadership and others to some form of subservience. Access to positions is rarely based upon individual ability but is institutionalized to such an extent that those who occupy positions of power and privilege do so either because of some form of ascribed status or because of institutionalized forms of advantage that give them the opportunity to achieve status. It is this institutionalized nature of the hierarchical structure that predetermines which individuals or groups will prevail and which ones will be subservient. It is also through such institutionalized differentials that those who have accrued power and privilege are able to acquire still further power and privilege for themselves and for those they have selected to inherit their positions.

One of the means by which this order is supported and reinforced has been to insure that women have no legitimate means of changing or managing the institutions that define and maintain their subordination. Confining women in the home, banning them from meaningful positions outside the family, and excluding them from the bench and the pulpit is to deny them the means of bringing about change in their status. The best they can hope for is a merciful master both inside and outside the home.

The maintenance of such a hierarchical order and the continuation of the authority and advantage of the few is to some extent dependent upon its 'acceptance' by the many. It is the patriarchal ideology that serves to reinforce this acceptance. The ideology is supportive of the principle of a hierarchical order, as opposed to an egalitarian one, and of the hierarchy currently in power. It is a rationalization for inequality and serves as a means of creating acceptance of subordination by those destined to such positions.

The ideology insures that internal controls regulate the complaints of most subordinates. Socialization into an acceptance of the 'rightful' nature of the order and its inequities can, if successful, allow such inequities to go unquestioned and unchallenged or to make challenges seem unnatural or immoral. Such a general acceptance of the hierarchical structure means that any challenges to it (from those who are not internally controlled by the idea of its rightfulness) will be met by external constraints in the guise of social pressures to conform (from those who do believe in its rightfulness) and by legitimate intervention both to prevent and to punish deviance. When the ideology legitimizes the order and makes it right, natural, and sacred, the potential conflict inherent in all hierarchies is more likely to produce conflict within the individual and less likely to emerge as overt resistance.

From: Emerson Dobash and Russell Dobash, *Violence Against Wives: A Case Against the Patriarchy.* New York: Free Press, 1979, pp. 43-44.

to maintain his power within the family and keep the woman in her place. Dobash and Dobash summarize this view (1979:21):

"The family historically has operated and continues to operate for the benefit of men and the state and rarely for women." As the legal specifications for the subjection of the women have gradually lessened, men have resorted to force in order to maintain their position of privilege.

Increasingly sociological studies correlate wife abuse with the lack of resources, negative institutional response, and traditional ideology fostered by patriarchy (Pagelow, 1981; Bowker, 1983a). The institutions of society systematically neglect and trap women in the abusive relationship, as well as give sanction to the man's violence. In fact, the helping agencies are few in number and often antagonistic in nature. Therefore, battered women subject to their husbands' violent "strategy of control" are not passive nor provocative; rather they are confined by lack of alternatives (Bowker and McCallum, 1982; Schechter, 1982). Bowker's study (1983a) of battered women who managed to stop the abuse showed that women actively attempt to stop their husbands' violence rather than passively submit to it. The women continuously developed strategies to "beat wife beating" until they found a combination of things that finally worked.

Violent Culture Versus Patriarchal Society

The debate between social learning and sociopolitical theorists is intense, since each emphasizes different fundamental causes that imply different modes of treatment, as outlined in Chapter 1. The social learning theorists tend to trace the wife abuse sociologically to a violent culture. The sociopolitical proponents see the family violence rooted in the patriarchal society. Both positions, nevertheless, assert that wife abuse is an outgrowth of society at large and must ultimately be addressed as an ingrained social problem.

Researchers like Straus, Gelles, and Steinmetz have famously forwarded the violent culture interpretation with their broad empirical data. As mentioned, this team of sociologists in their national survey of over 2000 families observe family violence to be an outgrowth of the violence taught, sanctioned, and even glorified in our society. As they explain in *Behind Closed Doors* (1980:44).

> At the same time, the violence *by* wives uncovered in this study suggests that a fundamental solution to the problem of wife-beating has to go beyond concern with how to control assaulting husbands. It seems that violence is built into the very structure of the society and the family system itself. . . . It is only one aspect of the general pattern of family violence, which includes partner-child violence, child-to-child violence, and wife-to-husband violence. To eliminate the particularly brutal form of violence known as wife-beating will require changes in the cultural system of violence on which so much of American society is based.

Roy (1982b) in her essay on the subject, "The Nature of Abusive Behavior," discusses the impact that pervasive social and political acts of violence have on family behavior. She suggests that social violence perpetuates a disregard, insensitivity, and brutality toward others. The escalation of nuclear weaponry, militarization of foreign affairs, reinstatement of the death penalty, hard-core pornography, sensationalized exploitation films and novels, dramatized terrorism on TV, and careless toxic waste disposal as a part of corporate policy, all tend to legitimate violence throughout society.

Stacey and Shupe (1983:196) conclude their domestic violence study of 542 case histories and 2096 telephone interviews with a similar indictment of the deep-seated violence in American society:

> . . . We think there is good reason to believe that a cult of violence is spreading throughout our society and affecting every sector. By "cult" we do not mean that it is an organized movement or conspiracy. Rather, it

is a cultural pattern, a trend. The glorification of violence in motion pictures, television, and books, and the electronic media's technical sophistication that shows us violence realistically but makes it exciting, contribute to this cult. But this is not the cause. The cult is an acceptance of violence, learning to expect it, to tolerate it and commit it, however much one dreads it. This cult is stimulated by a violent environment that affects each generation of men and women, making them even more desensitized to the problem.

Film attractions like "Return of the Jedi" to popular arcade games like "Missile Command" all have insidious consequences.

On the other hand, researchers like Dobash and Dobash (1979) and activists such as Schechter (1982) debunk the violent culture thesis as a diversion from the central issue of persistent violence against women in a patriarchy. Schechter (1982:209) surmises in her treatise:

Women abuse is viewed here as an historical expression of male domination manifested within the family and currently reinforced by the institutions, economic arrangements and sexist division of labor within capitalist society. Only by analyzing this total context of battering will women and men be able to devise a long-range plan to eliminate it.

These proponents of the sociopolitical theory press the question "why is such an inordinate amount of violence in society perpetrated against women?" Dobash and Dobash (1979:22) point out, in *Violence Against Wives*, that men are systematically socialized into violence as a problem-solving technique, more so than women, in order to maintain their privilege in a sexist society. They note:

Because violence against wives is so widespread and transcends the bounds of any particular social group, we do not consider the subculture of violence thesis an adequate explanation for this problem . . . All men see themselves as controllers of women, and because they are socialized into the use of violence, they are potential aggressors against their wives.

The notion of patriarchy, in fact, may be enacted most strongly—and perhaps most unconsciously—in the home. Even when men are intellectually sympathetic or tolerant of the women's struggle to gain equal employment opportunity, comparable pay, and political leadership, they often continue their role of domination and authority in the household (see Rubin, 1983). As Carlson (1978) observes in her account of wife abuse:

> Whatever our status or social habits . . . the family home has a tradition of its own. Part of this tradition has the husband and father as absolute ruler. Out of generosity he may give some of the power away. He may help with the dishes or help with the kids. But it is understood he doesn't have to do it; it is "helping"; it is a gift. His work is to maintain his version of a proper family. His wife and children must be trained to his standards of decorum. If he feels the need to use physical force to maintain the version, he has had considerable social support.

The dominate-submissive power relationships in the family are easily turned into violence, especially if the man feels his power and privilege being challenged (Finkelhor, 1983:18-19). Dobash and Dobash (1979:93) conclude:

> It cannot be stressed too much that it is marriage and the taking on the status of wife that make a woman the "appropriate victim" of violence aimed at "putting her in her place," and that differential marital responsibility and authority give the husband both the perceived right and the obligation to control his wife's behavior and thus the means to justify beating her.

The violent culture proponents, although sympathetic to the assertions of the patriarchal society adherents, consider their radical assertions as polemical rather than founded on an empirical basis of fact. They note that Dobash and Dobash's (1979) study of 3020 reported cases of violence in two Scottish cities is limited to police reports in a particular location. Whereas, the Straus, Gelles, and Steinmetz (1980) survey is of national scope and random in selection, even though it has its own failings as a method of data collection. Moreover, the latter research documents the incidence of wife-to-husband violence, as well as a web of family violence that extends to parent and child, child and child, parent and grandparent, and human to pet. According to violent culture proponents, the patriarchy proponents dogmatically attend to male violence against women; precluding some worthwhile and constructive efforts to mitigate the broader, more entangled social problem of domestic violence.

The patriachy proponents, contrarily, criticize the "violence" surveys for being "ahistorical," and "misogynist." The violent culture proponents ignore the legacy of women's subjection to men in the form of chattel, legal beating, or customary infidelity. Their consideration of child abuse with wife abuse also overlooks the different historical roots of each phenomena (Schechter, 1982:323-325). Furthermore, "Science itself is shaped by and reinforces the sexism in which it exists" (Wardell et al., 1983:80). Many of the social science surveys, therefore, despite their good intentions, suggest women play a role in their victimization. The critics insist that there is no conclusive empirical evidence for a victim-prone personality among women (Walker, 1983).

Furthermore, the violent culture proponents do not evaluate the impact or cause of the violent incidents recorded in their surveys (see Hilberman, 1981; Pleck et al., 1978). Acts of violence, even if equal in frequency, affect the sexes differently. A woman shoving a man, for example, cannot be equated with a man shoving a woman. Also, it may be that much of the recorded female violence is in self-defense or retaliation to the male dominance, control, or abuse. Whatever aggressive acts a woman might initiate are justifiable self-defense given the context of domestic oppression. Schechter (1982:23) explains "that violence cuts off all discussion, makes its victims fearful and intimidated, and graphically demonstrates 'who is boss.'" Lastly, the validity of the intergenerational transmission argument is contested. Dobash and Dobash (1979:154-159) note, for instance, that brothers raised in similar levels of violence are often not both violent toward their wives, and that the violence against women is so extensive it is difficult to assess personal variables.

Underlying debates about the causes of wife abuse is the issue of who in the family holds the responsibility for the acts of abuse. Clearly, the violent culture position suggests that the responsibility is shared between husband and wife. The patriarchal position holds that the man is decisively at fault. The latter, therefore, strongly criticizes the psychological and social learning theorists for promoting "naive and insidious provocation theories" that see women as inciting or provoking the violence themselves. Provocation theories diffuse the batterers' guilt and responsibility by suggesting that the wife asked to be hit. "She had it coming," explain many male batterers. This "blaming the victim," according to the patriarchal position, is a subtle way of justifying men's actions, neutralizing public outrage, and thus maintaining male authority (see Schechter, 1982:20-27, and Dobash and Dobash, 1979:133-137, for further discussion of provocation theories).

Men's Liberation

The men's movement, founded in the writings of Nichols (1974) and Farrell (1974), has brought some integration of these themes of violence and patriarchy through its examination of the male socialization and its consequences for men, as well as women. It forged the attention directed to the male sex role by the human potential and feminist movements to give men some self-interest in the on-going social change, as well. Men began to see that their rejection of feminine qualities in themselves limited their personal growth. In fact, as men began to turn their gaze inward, as the human potential movement urged, they found a very shallow and often empty personality. Their lack of human development led them to respond to others, especially women, in an immature and uncaring way, as the feminist movement so forcefully argued (see Farrell, 1974; Fasteau, 1974; Pleck and Sawyer, ed., 1974; Kosimar, 1976; Goldberg, 1976; Fein, 1977; Crites and Fitzgerald, 1978; Lewis, 1981; David and Brannon, ed., 1982; Ehrenreich, 1983; and Kiley, 1983).

As this movement has matured over the last several years, two factions have emerged with different emphasis. The Free Men liberationists, on the one hand, forward a therapeutic approach to helping men become more sensitive and expressive (see Goldberg, 1979). The National Organization for Chainging Men, on the other hand, encourages more of a social action approach to undo sexism (see Snodgrass, 1977). These groups, nonetheless, share some fundamental assumptions about the male sex role.

The Malignant Masculinity

In the men's movement analysis, men are debilitated by the spurious sense of masculinity held before them. The male role predicated on domination was ostensibly necessary at one time for survival. In the modern world, the survival-of-the-fittest notion has its drawbacks. For one, the invincible John Wayne role is largely unattainable. Physical toughness and fierceness is simply inadequate to command the complexities of a highly intricate, information-based, post-industrial society (Gerzon, 1982). If one is able to live up to the male role, he finds it frought with disconcerting contradictions (Pleck, 1981b). The Super Man is to be dispassionate, yet wildly romantic, in emotional control yet openly angry.

Consequently, being male is frought with frustration either for not fulfilling the idealized masculine role or from struggling with its irreconcilable extremes. This frustration, psychologists tell us, is translated into aggression, which in turn is often expressed as violence. In fact, men are taught to express aggression primarily as violence rather than through alternative modes of creativity, according to the spate of literature on male socialization.

The male sex role is dysfunctional in a more fundamental way, as well: it necessitates a denial of one's emotional feelings and physical sensations (Goldberg, 1976). The traditional male, in fact, becomes a dispassionate machine of mechanistic dimensions (Fasteau, 1974). In the competitive market place, one has to remain self-contained in order to appear invincible to his competitor. To express one's feelings is to be vulnerable and weak. The pressure to be unmoved by emotions becomes so intense that men begin to sacrifice all intimacy, spontaneity, and disclosure. Men become, in many cases, virtually inexpressive (Fein, 1977). As one becomes less feeling he can compete better; as the competition escalates, he becomes even more unfeeling, or so the scenario goes.

The traditional male, in the process, is left to define himself not from within but more from without. Most conveniently, he defines himself in terms of what he is against, or what he is not. As psychologist Herb Goldberg (1976:6) explains:

> Traditional masculinity is largely a psychological defensive operation rather than an authentic and organic process. A man's psychological energy is used to defend against, rather than to express, what he really is. His efforts are directed at proving to himself and others what he is not: Feminine, dependent, emotional, passive, afraid, helpless, a loser, a failure, impotent and so on. He burns himself out in this never-ending need to prove, because he can never sufficiently prove it. To his final day he is driven to project himself as "a man" whether on the battlefield, behind the desk, in lovemaking, on the hospital operating table, in a barroom or even on his death bed. And when he fails, his self-hate and humiliation overwhelm him. He would sooner die than acknowledge the things that threaten him most.

The feminine qualities of care, nurturance, and cooperation, therefore, are untenable to the independent male. In fact, one recent revision of cultural history shows the male's flight from commitment in general to be the cause of the breakdown of the family, the blame for which is usually attributed to radical feminists (Ehrenreich, 1983). Men, moreover, tend to disassociate themselves from feminity and despise it in other men. This aversion is often translated into an acute homophobia and a fear of relationships, affection, and even touching with other men. Of course, the accusation of "sissy" while growing up teaches boys to deny "feminine" feelings early on (Hartley, 1974) and engender a rejection of open relationships.

The male sex role creates, furthermore, an emotional "funnel system" (see Table 2-4), causing a wide range of emotions to be expressed as anger, rage, and violence. The unexpressed feelings store up until they erupt in the one emotion that is allowed for men—anger. This anger gets funnelled toward females in two ways: One, women who are more attuned to feelings often sense the pent up emotions of the men and try to call them out. In the process, they may become the target of violence. Two, men are forced to become aware of their feelings as they resonate with women's expressiveness; consequently, a man often perceives his spouse to be a threat to his emotional control.

Some men simply over-intellectualize as a means of avoiding their emotions and maintaining control. Their arm's length analysis keeps them aloof and uninvolved. It serves as an offense as well as a defense. A determination of categories and correlations helps men sort out individuals, predict their behavior and influence it for one's own benefit, rather than accept others openly or at face value. At its extreme, the detached judgments and anticipations can become a kind of psychological violence denying others the opportunity to be themselves.

The repressed male is, furthermore, destructive to himself (Goldberg, 1976; Harrison, 1978; Meinecke, 1981). He becomes so out of touch with his body that he actually abuses it. He accepts high levels of tension and stress in order to compete in business and the threat of severe injury to compete in sports. His lack of self care takes its toll in heart attacks, alcoholism, and suicide (all of which occur at a much higher rate for men than for women). The man also subjects himself to high risks in recreation and hazardous conditions on the job. In sum, his life span is eight years shorter than a woman's largely because of the

Table 2-4: The Male Emotional Funnel System

The task for men who want to change the old violent and abusive behaviors is to move from the traditional model on the right, where anger is the primary negative or difficult feeling, toward the left, where anger is but one of many clearly identified negative/difficult feelings. We must reclaim our right to the natural human emotiveness that is denied by the limits of traditional masculinity.

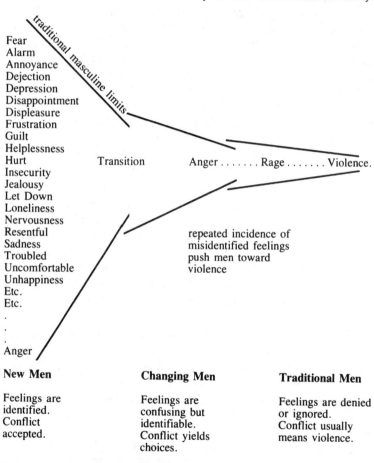

Fear
Alarm
Annoyance
Dejection
Depression
Disappointment
Displeasure
Frustration
Guilt
Helplessness
Hurt   Transition   Anger . . . . Rage . . . . Violence.
Insecurity
Jealousy
Let Down
Loneliness
Nervousness
Resentful
Sadness   repeated incidence of
Troubled   misidentified feelings
Uncomfortable   push men toward
Unhappiness   violence
Etc.
Etc.
.
.
.
Anger

New Men   **Changing Men**   **Traditional Men**

Feelings are   Feelings are   Feelings are denied
identified.   confusing but   or ignored.
Conflict   identifiable.   Conflict usually
accepted.   Conflict yields   means violence.
                         choices.

From: Don Long, RAVEN, St. Louis, MO.

Table 2-5: The Hazardous Male Role

Factors Defining the Male Role

I. "No Sissy Stuff": There is a stigma attached to anything even vaguely feminine;

II. "The Big Wheel": We need success, status and admiration;

III. "The Sturdy Oak": We strive for a manly air of toughness, confidence and self-reliance;

IV. "Give 'Em Hell": Masculinity thrives on an aura of aggression, violence and daring.

From: Robert Brannon and Deborah David, "The Male Sex Role: Our Culture's Blueprint for Manhood, and What It's Done for Us Lately," in David and Brannon, *The Forty-Nine Percent Majority*. Reading, MA: Addison Wesley, 1979.

How The Male Role Is Hazardous To Men's Health

1. Aggressiveness and competitiveness cause men to put themselves in dangerous situations.

2. Emotional inexpressiveness causes psychosomatic and other health problems.

3. Men take greater risks.

4. Men's jobs expose them to physical danger.

5. Men's jobs expose them to psychological stress.

6. The male role socializes men to have personality characteristics associated with high mortality (e.g. type "A" behavior and your heart).

7. Responsibilities as family breadwinners expose men to psychological stress.

8. The male role encourages certain specific behaviors that endanger health, specifically tobacco smoking and alcohol consumption.

9. The male role psychologically discourages men from taking adequate medical care of themselves.

10. The male role discourages men from seeking counseling and other psychological help.

From: Joseph Pleck, *The Myth of Masculinity*. Boston, MA: M.I.T. Press, 1981.

masculine role he assumes (see Table 2-5). The bodily denial and neglect becomes a kind of self-hate, in fact. A former roughneck on oil rigs reflects on the dangerous work and the reckless lifestyle:

> To be so contemptuous of our health and safety, we must first of all be afflicted with a contempt for self, a conviction that our lives are worth almost nothing. When men get to the point where approval can only be won by destroying ourselves, then we are really caught. Because the more we destroy ourselves, the more we prove that we are worthless—so the more we need to destroy ourselves . . . .(Stodder, 1979:41).

Many critics of the male role have traced, in fact, the destructiveness throughout the world to men obsessed with masculinity (see Stone, 1974). Sexual politics is at least partly to blame for the foreign policy fiascos such as the Bay of Pigs invasion. As Gerzon (1982:92) summarizes the evidence: "Bellicose men of action advocated toughness and dissenters were afraid of looking soft. . . In foreign affairs everything seems to become a test of our manhood." (see also Jamus et al., 1977.)

Etheredge (1978) studied 126 foreign service officers of the State Department to reach a similar conclusion. He found the officers to be highly ambitious, competitive, willing to use force, and emotionally inadequate—sometimes neurotically so. Yet their foreign policy decisions were cloaked in an air of rationality and objectivity. The threat of nuclear annihilation, of course, makes the masculine "one-upmanship" intolerable. It leads Gerzon (1982:83), in his historical review of male images, to assert that the traditional male ideal may be at a historical dead end: "The masculine traits that formerly assured survival will now, if not balanced by the feminine, assure destruction."

Male-Female Sex Roles

At the heart of this argument is the notion that men and women are socialized into conflicting roles. Their learned differences make conflicts inevitable. The man's socialization into a masculine role causes him to respond to conflict in the way he knows best—with violence. The absence of violence in a relationship is therefore the result of the two partners in a perfunctory way living separate lives, risking a lack of fulfillment, or moving beyond the sex role boundaries to a genuine sharing of emotions and power (Rubin, 1983).

One sociologist, Janes Henslin (1981:62), reflecting on his own socialization as a man, noted the implications of sex role differences and the contradictions they imply for relationships:

> Hardly any of this process of becoming a man in our society augurs well for marriage. The separateness of the world that we males join at birth signals our embarkation on an intricate process whereby we become a different type of being. Our world differs in most all aspects from the world of females. Not only do we look different, not only do we talk and act differently, but our total orientation to life sharply contrasts with theirs. Yet we are expected to unite permanently with someone from the contradispositional world and, in spite of these basic and essential differences, share not only a life space, but also bring together our goals, hopes, dreams, aspirations, and other "stuff" of which life is made.

> Is it any wonder that, in perhaps the typical case, men remain strangers to women and women to men?

The psychology of women *is* different from men, but not inferior to it, as many recent feminist reassessments of female development have shown. Gilligan (1982) documents the different frame of reference between men and women. Women interpret moral dilemmas, for instance, based on relationship and care, rather than achievement and fairness as men more often do. This sort of evidence leads Gilligan (1982:173) to a conclusion similar to Henslin's personal observation: "My research suggests that men and women may speak different languages that they assume are the same, using similar words to encode disparate experiences of self and social relationships."

The assessments of the masculine role are particularly indict-
ing. They characterize the typical man as isolated from others,
especially women. The masculinity, in fact, is a kind of
psychological defense mechanism shielding us from encounters
that would expose our insecurities. As Goldberg (1979:9) surmizes
from his clinical practice and study:

> The repression of emotion, the denial and suppression
> of vulnerability, the compulsive competitiveness, the
> fear of losing, the anxiety over touching or any other
> form of sensual display, the controlled intellectualizing,
> and the general lack of spontaneity and unselfconscious
> playfulness serve to make the companionship of most
> men unsatisfying and highly limited. Men are at their
> best when a task is to be completed, a problem solved,
> or an enemy battled. Without such a structure, however,
> anxiety and self-consciousness accelerate too rapidly
> to allow for a sustained pleasurable experience.

This separatist posture is ironically accentuated in loving relationships. The idealized playboy is inexpressive and unemotional
as he uses women for his own pleasure and status. He has learned
through back seat courtship to maneuver women to submit to his
sexual whim. According to one exposé, men are left with little
alternative, considering their socialization. Their repression of emotion and denial of feeling leads them to objectify the world around
them, including women (see Litewka, 1979). Even the male's
genitals are considered "things."

Women, in essence, become objects also to be managed,
manipulated, or collected by men. As objects, they are admired
for parts of their bodies on which men fixate, rather than develop
a relationship with the whole person. "I am an ass man . . . or
a leg man," is the common claim. The only relationship left in
the male-created world is to "have" something. One cannot share
and interrelate to "things"; therefore, men are left to conquer
them—that is, put them in their domain of control and possess them.

It is no accident, according to this analysis, that sexuality is
cast as some sort of competitive sport where each man tries to

"bag" more women and better looking women than the other. Men talk in terms of "hunting," "trapping," and "scoring"— all as part of a big game. They consequently are left to perform as an athlete in demonstrating their potency and manliness. Ironically, it is this self-conscious preoccupation with performance that leads to sexual impotency. When women do become assertive and expressive, usurping some of the male's role or challenging it with emotional intimacy, the likelihood of impotency increases (see Rubin, 1979).

Sexuality, moreover, can be confused with the drive for power. In the process, sex can become a violent act, and violence can be seen as sexual. The intermingling of sex, power, and violence, as is done in movies like *Friday the 13th* and in the epidemic of rapes, is revealed frighteningly in the account of one Viet Nam veteran (Frank, 1981:3):

> You are the hunter. And there is incredible, just this incredible sense of power in killing five people . . . ah, between the two of us it was five people. And the only way I can equate it is to ejaculation. Just an incredible sense of relief, you know, that I did this. I was very powerful. . . .

The traditional "breadwinner" role, moreover, reinforces this sense of detachment in adult life. As the provider of the family, men feel it their duty to compete for material gain and to see their success in terms of their family's status and appearance, rather than its bonds and attitudes (Cobb and Sennett, 1973). The family becomes another thing—a kind of trophy—for being male. Others suggest that the position of the man in the workplace accentuates the objectification process in the home (Shepard, 1977). The business or factory life requires men to be productive, efficient, and regimented. When the man returns to his family at the end of the day, he tends, therefore, to manage his wife and children as he does his work.

The male's difficulty in forming relationships extends to other men as well as women. Paradoxically, it may be the male's lack of intimacy and prevalent loneliness that underlie the penchant to join all male clubs, teams, business organizations. According to

Tiger (1969), men throughout history and across cultures have joined together in groups. This tendency, in Tiger's analysis, is biologically based. In fact, it essential to bring organization and direction to society. More recent assessments of male relationships, however, see the clubiness as a superficial protection of power and substitute for intimacy. Men are shown, for instance, to turn to women for emotional support and encouragement rather than to their male counterparts (Komarovsky, 1975; see also Kiley, 1983).

Therapy for Males

What can be done about the inherently malignant and violent male sex role? Pleck's (1981a) thorough examination of the research on masculinity confirms the assertions of the men's liberation movement. He debuncks the "male sex role identity" that suggests masculinity is psychologically or biologically innate in favor of "sex role stress" in which identity is adopted through social approval and situational adaption. In other words, our sense of masculinity is learned from society. We have the innate potential, then, to be free of its burdens, contradictions, and shortcomings. As Pleck (1981b:77) explains:

> Exaggerated masculinity, rather than being a reaction to inner insecurities, may reflect an overlearning of the externally prescribed role or an over conformity to it. The alternative interpretation, part of the emerging new theory of sex-role strain, puts the burden of responsibility for destructive, extreme male behavior on society's unrealistic male-role expectations—where it belongs—and not on the failings of individual men and their mothers.

Goldberg's (1979) writings on the self-care for men advocate a gestalt kind of therapy that confronts men with their feelings and sensations. In the spirit of the human potential movement, Goldberg guides men toward exploring themselves and their capacities for caring and nurturing. There is, of course, a personal pain involved in putting on the "new man." According to Goldberg, the strongest barriers to this opening are the shame, guilt, and self-hatred that men have accepted as part of their sex role. As the door swings open, the confrontation with the shallowness and the rush of emotion causes a state of depression. Support groups or consciousness raising groups for men have, therefore, sprung up to help facilitate and ease this transition.

Some more radical men, however, question the self-indulgent aspects of this form of men's liberation (see Snodgrass, ed., 1977). The "we are victims, too!" theme smacks of naiveté. Men are handsomely rewarded with power, wealth, and prestige for their self-containment and competitiveness. As Sattel (1976:476) notes: "Male inexpressiveness is instrumental in maintaining positions of power and privilege for men." There are many more rewards for remaining "pent-up" than there are punishments—namely, men get money and power by being hard-nosed and aggressive. What ultimately has to be addressed, therefore, is the sexist system that makes it so beneficial for men to be unfeeling and ruthless. This will require astute political action to unseat the entrenched elite benefactors, not merely the sense of "feeling good" about oneself that comes from therapy.

Gerzon (1982) perhaps charts a middle ground. He advocates rethinking our masculinity as a means of becoming more responsible for ourselves. It will make us less likely to blame others for our shortcomings. He cautions, however, that the traditional images of manhood (the frontiersman, soldier, breadwinner, expert, and lord) are archetypes that grip our subconscious being. "These archetypes, or hero images, influence our behavior whether we are aware of it or not . . . . These images of manhood cannot be dislodged simply by frenetic consciousness raising or alternative lifestyles" (Gerzon, 1982:4).

There must be a personal and social pursuit of a new model of masculinity (the healer, mediator, companion, colleague, nurturer). As Pleck (1981a) points out, this search is not a matter of making women and men the same, but doing less to make them so different. Neither is it a matter of simply replacing one stereotypic role for another. The new man is likely to be discovered from within but achieved from without. It is a response to the diverse individualities of man and an establishment of the freedom of choice to be a different person. The new man, therefore, will take many forms.

Gerzon (1982:238) outlines the implications of this diversification on family relationships:

> As these emerging masculinities gain strength, men will no longer feel compelled to keep masculine and feminine roles separate. We can allow them to be shared. The lines of responsibility, such as his for making money or hers for taking care of the children, can soften. Most jobs are more rewarding if they are freely chosen and do not consume one's whole life. Men will be more balanced breadwinners if that responsibility is shared. Women will be more balanced caretakers if that responsibility, too, is shared. And as couples may wish to reverse roles completely; others may retain clearly divided roles. But if the freedom to choose is increased that outcome, whatever its form, will be liberating for both men and women.

This new direction, nevertheless, is largely uncharted and risky. Goldberg (1983) laments in his most recent book, for instance, the conflicts faced by liberated couples. There are, nonetheless, some indicators that suggest that relationships where decision-making is shared are less violent than where authoritarian decisions prevail (Straus et al., 1980:193-196), and children nurtured by both parents seem to be less inclined toward violence (Dinnerstein, 1979). It is of course too early to determine the impact of changing sex roles on the social phenomenon of wife abuse. There is clear evidence, however, that the male sex role stereotype contributes to the high incidence of family violence and may make all men potential batterers.

3

Men Fighting For Control

As the previous chapter suggests, much of the research and theory on men who batter, however helpful, offers generalizations about people we hardly know. At best, we assert that batterers have several characteristics that distinguish them as "deviant" individuals, yet they also display characteristics common to men in general. As the work with men who batter advances, there will, no doubt, be more heard from men who batter and men in general about their violent behavior. But more empathy for the man's position may also be a prerequisite for abuser programs. The more we grasp the experience of men who batter, the more likely they will be to accept treatment and to develop the desire to change. As Fleming (1979:308) explains in her broad overview of programs for battered women:

> Critical to working with abusive men is finding a basis
> for identification with them, their goals, aspirations,
> frustrations and being empathetic with their plight. In
> general, men are conditioned to believe that the need
> for counseling or therapy is a sign of weakness or inade-
> quacy, so that it is vital to establish a basis for trust . . .

This chapter begins with several profiles of abusers to help illustrate the perspective of men who batter and promote the empathy for which Fleming calls. My clinical interviews with men who batter, reveal batterers to be less domineering and less deficient than the prevailing research and theory suggest (Gondolf, in press). This is not to say that some batterers are not pitifully emasculated, hypermasculine, or ruthlessly exploitive, but that there is perhaps a more pervasive characterization to consider. As discussed in the second half of this chapter, the men portrayed here appear basically to be oversocialized into a traditional male role predicated on control. They exhibit more rigidity than outright aggressiveness or women hatred. The men in general appear to develop overbearing expectations for themselves and their wives. In failing to fulfill these imposing expectations, the men become frustrated and violent. This tendency appears to be the outgrowth of severe discipline and previous abuse that engendered self-hate or self-doubts. They reassert their sense of self-worth through compulsive control—control that gives them some sense of being in charge and, therefore, of being "somebody." This issue of control has important implications for how we interpret wife abuse and how we deal with it, as the conclusion suggests. Helping men to simply "control themselves" may not only be insufficient but add to the problem. Men who batter need to "let go" of some of that control.

Five Profiles

All the men in the profiles have participated from two weeks to one year in a program for men who batter. Although the extent and nature of their violence differ, the men are all what might be termed the "everyday" type of batterer. They include a steel worker, an unemployed mill laborer, a graduate student, a delivery driver, and a sales representative—all who, despite their calm demeanor, "go off the handle" as much as once every month to every week. Their behavior is frequently physically harmful; it includes intermittent shoves or punches and kicks in the back that hospitalized a spouse for weeks.

Their battering, moreover, is chronic in nature, following "the cycle of violence" outlined by Lenore Walker in *The Battered*

Women (1979). Tensions build until the man explodes into violence. The abusive incident is followed usually by a period of remorse and apologies which lead both partners to suspect that the violent behavior is past. However, tensions begin to mount once again and before long the violence is repeated (see Table 3-1). Consequently, the men appear like Dr. Jekyll and Mr. Hyde confusing themselves and their wives. In most cases, the husband and wife both wish to look at the Dr. Jekyll or "good" side which prevails most of the time, despite Mr. Hyde's unexpected intrusions.

The "everyday type" of batterers portrayed here, admittedly, represents only a portion—but the most common kind (approximately 75%)—of the batterers at large. Program staff estimate that about 5% to 10% of all batterers comprise a "sadistic" type who commits bizarre and brutal acts of sexual and physical violence to others as well as their wives. Another 10% to 15% of all batterers comprise a "stress" type. Their battering, however severe, is more the result of momentary crisis rather than an ingrained personality defect. When the acute stress over being fired or loss of a loved one subsides, the abuse does also (see also Pagelow, 1981:101).

The majority of men who batter, therefore, are not unlike those in the following profiles. They come from a vast cross section of classes and occupations and display a diversity of personality temperaments and styles. Some drink heavily, others not at all. There are church goers and non-church goers. But, as suggested in the profiles, they appear universally to be responding to their feelings of desperation with punishing control.

Bill, the lover of children

Bill is a deceptively sensitive and caring man within his formidable stature (6 ft. 6 in., 230 lbs.). Unfortunately he has

Table 3-1: Getting Out of the Violence Cycle

Introduction: The following diagram represents the usual three-stage cycle of violence (solid lines) and the ways men drift back into the cycle after attempting to stop their violence (dashed lines). Also, the steps to break the cycle are indicated (asterisks). Men most often look for help soon after a violent episode, but are often easily fooled into thinking that they are better before making substantial changes. As suggested in the diagram, several additional steps are needed to successfully break the cycle.

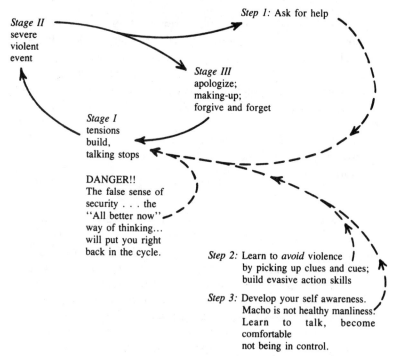

Stage II
severe
violent
event

Step 1: Ask for help

Stage III
apologize;
making-up;
forgive and forget

Stage I
tensions
build,
talking stops

DANGER!!
The false sense of
security . . . the
"All better now"
way of thinking...
will put you right
back in the cycle.

Step 2: Learn to *avoid* violence
by picking up clues and cues;
build evasive action skills

Step 3: Develop your self awareness.
Macho is not healthy manliness.
Learn to talk, become
comfortable
not being in control.

Step 4: Learn to *prevent* Stage I.
Learn to accept anger; through
clear communication, a community of
friends and a new self concept.

From: RAVEN, St. Louis, Mo.

"a temper which just snaps" and leads him to do something "stupid," namely hurt someone dear to him. He explains frequently how much he loves his family—his second wife and four stepchildren. His 13-year-old son of his first marriage is, too, a big part of his life. It is this son who has given him "a reason for going on" during the recent separation from his present wife. Bill adds that he "loves kids" in general and for a long while was interested in adopting more or becoming a Big Brother.

Ironically, he has hurt most of those he professes to love so much. During the five years of marriage to his second wife, Bill has frequently abused the four stepchildren, ages 8 to 16, and his wife. As often as once a month, he has verbally attacked any one of them, but insists that he "slapped one in the face only once." However, he did strike his younger daughter with a pool stick across her back and severely bruised her. She accidently broke the cue during a pool game in their basement, and Bill, "punishing her for her carelessness," overreacted.

Bill and his wife have had arguments as often as twice a month, although his wife insists it's more often. Bill and his wife argue loud and forcefully. "She gives it back as hard to me as I give it to her." His wife, as Bill concedes, is trying to help him, but he simply explodes. In most fights, he would eventually grab his 5 ft. 2 in. wife by the arm or wrist "with the force sufficient to yank it off at the socket." But Bill insists that he never struck her as he has the children, even though his wife claims that he has on occasion.

As suggested, the children are at the heart of many of the disagreements. Bill believes "the children should obey him and their mother," and if they do not, he will whip them with a leather belt down in the basement. "That's part of being a good father," explains Bill. His wife, however, is adamant in her notions about how children should be raised. Because of her strong religious beliefs, she objects to stern discipline or supervision. For instance, when the oldest son does work for Bill, Bill does not pay him in cash but rather will take the son on a trip or to a movie; whereas, the wife thinks that her son should be paid and use the money as he wishes. Bill notes that he has tried to talk with his stepchildren about his disagreements with his wife over his approach to them, but to no avail. "They obviously did not appreciate my side of the story," relents Bill.

To compound problems the children's real father recently started visiting them again after no contact for seven years. Consequently, Bill feels that he is being "pushed aside by this person, after all my efforts to be affectionate to them." Bill took the children camping and to the amusement park, for example, and "showed them so much attention that my wife began to feel neglected." Bill strongly disapproved of the children's visiting their natural father "who paid them no attention for all this time." However, his wife, who had been brutally beaten by this first husband, insists that seeing their natural father is the "right thing to do." Bill's wife says that Bill ought to support the visitation, considering the poor relationship that Bill had with his natural father.

Bill had been separated from his wife for nearly a month by the time he contacted the counseling program for men who batter. His wife and the children left home one day to live with her mother while Bill was at work, because the children had told her of more beatings and she had experienced a recent bout herself. "I was simply afraid that I would come home some day from my job and find the children dead," explained Bill's wife. With an "order of protection" in hand, she pressed Bill to move to his aunt's residence and returned to the family house with the children. She also firmly threatened to have him put in jail if he "so much as talked to her or the children." Furthermore, Bill's wife initiated divorce proceedings shortly after leaving him.

Bill fell into severe depression after "losing so much." "There were times I just wanted to drive head-on into a tree." He became, as he says, "very nervous and unable to sleep." He found himself smoking again, but continued not to drink or use drugs. His dejection was in part over "not doing something four or five years ago before it was too late." But Bill always believed he should "work it out on his own." Consequently, he resisted the encouragement to see a psychologist, a fact he mentioned at least twice during his intake interview. Finally, he sought help in a familiar place; he returned to the church he had attended as a youth. "I approached the minister about my problem," Bill reports, and the minister called the women's shelter for referral to a men's program.

Calling the program hotline was "the most difficult thing I ever did," he says, but Bill was "determined to do something about the problem this time." Bill in fact drove around the initial meeting place twice before parking and coming in. As soon as he sat down, however, he started talking pausing only to hold back some tears. He concluded by vowing to join the program and "do whatever is necessary—attend meetings for two years if need be." As he says these words Bill hits the table repeatedly with his six inch fist.

Much of Bill's abusive behavior is a repeat of his childhood. On his own initiative, Bill recalls his real father beating him and his sister as punishment for minor things. Bill was "slugged" once for using his fork instead of his spoon at the dinner table, and another time he had his ear twisted until he licked up the milk he had spilled on the floor. Bill reflects on his alcoholic father's harshness:

> You knew when my father shook his finger at you that you better listen or get smacked. When he came home one day he smacked even my best friend and cracked the wall with my mother. The worst though was when he tied up me and my sister with shoe strings and proceeded to wipe the house up with my mother. We would go to bed and she would utterly come flying through the door without opening it.

> One time my father came home drunk and started throwing my sister and mother around. So I went and got a butcher knife and told him that he better stop. He said that I'd better use it or he'd kill me. Fortunately, my sister came in and pulled him away before he did anything and left me standing their shaking for an hour. (To this day I shake like that when I get scared.) The thing that surprised me the most, though, was that when

I went to my mother for sympathy she just told me, "Do
what your father says; his word is law."

Bill's mother eventually divorced and remarried, but Bill's
new stepfather was also "a very stern man" who whipped or
punched Bill as punishment. Bill explains that he has flashes of
these childhood experiences when he is abusive. In fact, it is the
memories of his mother being hit that keep him from beating his
wife more severely.

Bill went into the army in 1962 as soon as he completed high
school. He was "always being yelled at, just like at home, but
this time because I was so tall." As Bill notes, "I stood out from
the rest of the group and suffered for it." He took an electronics
course but "regrettably" never furthered his education beyond
that. His first marriage to a hometown girl was a "fluke." "We
both were not ready for it."

Bill sadly recollects his first child screaming as a baby and
his hitting the child as hard as he could; bruising him severely.
Bill was also abusive to his first wife, until she threatened him
with a gun and police arrest. He felt the abusive behavior had finally
passed with his first divorce. Within two years, he remarried to
a woman whom he met in the Parents-Without-Partners organization. A few months later, he was battering his wife once again.

Bill says he "hates" his job at the steel plant where he has
worked for over twelve years. After two operations, one on each
hand, to correct the damage done during years of labor, Bill is
beginning to reevaluate the impact of his working conditions on
his life:

The work is just plain brutal at times. There's no way you
can slow down or relax your body. You can't tell me there
is; why in the summer heat we had last year, when it was
103° outside; it felt like twice that in the mill. You couldn't
touch the building it was so hot. And you try and ask for
a break . . . forget it! It's eight hours pay and eight hours

work. We would have given anything to go outside and cool down, but no way. That's not in the schedule.

The EPA will come by for a noise check once in a while, but that just means the company bosses turn things down for that day. There are times you can be standing from here to that window (eight feet) from 3,000 degree molten steel. You can actually see your little silver suit smoking. And when they fire that furnace, it's like having a trumpet blow in your ear. A one million amp charge is used to spark it. You can feel the ground shake it's so strong! I mean there is heat and noise in there that you can't believe. It's impossible to concentrate or calm down nice. Of course, you're going to go home and play havoc on the family after some of those days.

Besides being unnerved by the heat and noise, Bill also complains of a foreman who "gets on his case" regularly. Nevertheless, the pay and benefits are good and other jobs are scarce.

As Bill grows out of his depression through the group support, he begins to shift more of the blame for the abuse to his wife and women in general. He can't understand why there is not more assistance for men in positions like his:

I mean it burns me some. Look where I am now. I have had two houses and two marriages. It's probably cost me $100,000. And here I am with a car that doesn't work half of the time and $16.00 in my pocket. You know it's hard to let all that go by—I mean just forget about it. I got nothing! You know that makes you feel like nothing some of the time . . . I could botch anything up.

As Bill's commitment to the program deepens, however, he becomes more relaxed and questioning of his "rights." He sees himself backing off in disputes at work and with his former family members. A year after the divorce, he and his most recent wife are remarried and remain together free of violence.

Joe, a quiet good guy

Joe who characterizes himself as shy and quiet, speaks softly and slowly when he explains his abusive relationship. His second wife and young child have left him, this time for good. "It hurts real bad to have her gone—and over one argument." It is not the first time that she has left him "over arguments," however. Joe has come home at least twice before to find a letter telling him that his wife had left because he was being "so mean." On the previous occasion, Joe tracked her down and "made up."

His wife went to a women's shelter for several weeks the second time. Joe visited her on the weekends first at a local restaurant and then at a near-by hotel. After the third visit, as Joe explains, he simply did not let his wife return to the shelter and took her home. "Each time she went back to the shelter, it was like she'd left me all over again." Within three months, she and the child were gone again. "I guess I just forced her to leave the shelter before she was ready," relents Joe. (Typically, Joe attended a men's program for a short period, while his wife was in the shelter but stopped attending as soon as he got his wife back home.)

During the summer while Joe was laid off from work, he and his wife decided to play cards, but had a disagreement over the rules. "She started arguing over nothing, so I grabbed her by the arm and told her to forget it." He admits to "yanking her pretty hard and giving her perhaps a bit of a shove." As Joe continues to recall the situation, "then she got hysterical and started to run for the neighbors." Only when pressed does he admit, "I may have slapped her just to try to bring her to her senses." His wife broke loose and did manage to reach the neighbors. Joe went inside to wait for her, but she did not return alone. The police arrived, escorted her to get her clothes, and took her and the child to the shelter.

According to Joe, poor communication is at the root of the problem. Joe points out:

I remember being at work and expecting to come home and find the house clean, dinner on the table, and my wife with her pants off waiting for me. I get there to find just the opposite. The house is a mess, and the last thing my wife wants is to go to bed. I realize now that she couldn't read my mind. I had all these expectations that were bound to make me disappointed when I got home.

Joe's battered wife had been leery about talking to him for sometime "for fear of setting him off." Joe's expressionless face was hard to read; therefore, she had no bearings, until his limits were reached and he had a fit of violence. "The anger leads to violence before you know it," observes Joe. "It just takes over and you become a different person." Joe's wife unfortunately bore the brunt of this "different person." "She thought I was about to kill her at least on five occasions." Joe admits throwing her down on the bed after she danced with another man one night in a bar. He recalls another fight in which she told him that she lost her love for him when he threw her first child over the fence because she was crying. Joe claims that he was just "wrestling with the kid because I wanted her to grow up tough." Joe, in fact, sees himself as fairly considerate. He does not "mind doing the dishes once in a while, but just not all the time."

Joe's wife had previously been married twice, once to "a guy who took her money and left" and to a truck driver who "gave her the time by herself that she needed." With a young daughter from a previous marriage, and now pregnant with Joe's child, she was living in a one room apartment in another town. She called Joe apparently to inform him of the divorce which she had filed against him, but would not disclose her number or residence, much to Joe's dismay.

Joe's wife continued to call Joe about once a week with varying degrees of resentment and affection, according to Joe. On two occasions, she accused Joe of being out with other women when she phoned earlier and found him not at home. Ironically, the one date arranged by a friend in over a year of separation was a "failure." Joe was so nervous prior to the foursome dinner date that he wanted to back out. "During the date, I couldn't even talk and so the woman must have thought I was a dud," recounts Joe.

Joe wrote his wife long apologetic letters expressing his faithfulness and love but she would not respond. She told him on the phone that it was because whatever she wrote could be used against her in court. Joe, desperate for some reconciliation, persisted. Her "being nice" in some of their two hour phone calls made Joe think they could get back together. When his wife continued to press for divorce, Joe assumed that his wife's mother did not like him and was "forcing her daughter to get a divorce." Perhaps they could get back together after the divorce, Joe then thought.

After the baby was born, Joe was permitted to visit every other week at the mother-in-law's residence for an hour. The time together was filled with friendly small talk but no mention of getting back together—an observation that baffled and depressed Joe. Consequently, Joe spent most of his evenings at a bar shooting pool and trying to pick up odd jobs.

Joe, like Bill, relates some of his present family problems to his own growing up. In his lower moments he talks about his father who "always put me down and made me feel stupid." His father, for instance, criticized him for missing squirrels when he hunted in the back yard. He refused to attend Joe's second wedding remarking, "You messed up one marriage, and now you are going to mess up another." More recently, Joe bought an old car from a friend at the bar, and his father upon seeing it "laughed at me and told me, I had been taken."

Joe's father always had his own way, according to Joe. His mother "still has to chop wood and really work for him." As Joe explains:

My father ruled the house. His word was law. My mother would always say, "You will have to wait until we talk to your father," or if I did something wrong, "Wait until your father comes home." He did what he wanted. He would paint the house pink, if he felt like it, and you'd better like it or else . . . .

I don't know where his money went. He had a good paying job. The only money I ever got was from my mother and she worked two jobs to support us kids.

Moreover, his father "never used to listen very well to other people." Joe notes that he has not communicated very well with his wife either. They have communicated best when she was at the shelter or over the phone.

As a youngster, Joe followed the crowd of his four older brothers. "I guess I had to prove myself sometimes," he recalls when discussing the numerous fights he had been in. Less than two years ago, Joe was in a fight not unlike those of his younger days. In an argument over a pool game, he was stabbed but managed to "run down" the combatant with his truck. Joe relates, too, that he fought with his first wife who "pushed me to my limit until I finally left." As Joe reports:

We'd used to have arguments over what I'd buy. I would buy the best there is. I'd tell her to look at the TV—it has lasted 10 years. You buy the best and it will last longer. But no, she'd want to get something cheap that wouldn't last a darn. So we'd get into a fight.

Feeling down and out for being laid off, finding no work, and having to live with his brother's family, Joe continues to be depressed and sullen. Joe explains:

Sometimes I just feel tired. I just don't have any purpose. When I had my job, I'd go to work at the mill and that's about it. I don't have any hobbies to speak of. Usually, I'd come home and all I can do is watch TV or go to bed. After 7 years of working there, there was just more of the same. I really don't have much to look forward to . . . even if I do get a job. That's why I get to thinking about just leaving—of taking off and going someplace to start all over again. Really—why not?

However, in the group meetings that he sporadically attends, Joe becomes more and more expressive. Instead of speculating constantly about how his wife feels and what she must be thinking about him, he communicates decisively about how he is feeling. He finally concedes that his wife deserves to have the divorce without his contesting it. Joe concludes:

> I guess I'll just have to find someone else. But this time I know you have to decide things together. The tradition of the man always being the head of the house is over. Everybody has their rights now.

Dan, the ambitious student

Dan, rather than down and out, is up and coming. He is a former VISTA worker and sociology undergraduate who is now studying in a graduate program in urban studies. He is short but well-built, and bearded with longish, well-groomed hair. He appears intense, analytical, and intelligent with a keen awareness of his own problems as well as others.

Dan has been living with a woman with whom he worked in VISTA for four years. He explains that they "had fights from the start." So they went their separate ways after the VISTA service and "tried to make it" at their respective homes. When jobs did not pan out, they gravitated to the university where Dan was admitted to a graduate program and his woman friend to undergraduate classes. She was not "that serious about school," however, and was bothered by tension headaches.

The two are now kept together, according to Dan, because of financial dependence on each other. His scholarship and loan pay for the apartment and her vehicle gets them around. "It is a relationship of circumstance," surmises Dan. Dan and his woman friend have "had fun together and good times," but Dan concedes that he is not sure where the relationship is headed. He says that he loves her but is not sure that they are compatible, especially when she resists his efforts "to help her improve." Moreover, Dan observes that there is "a monster inside him" that sometimes overturns his feelings of affection.

Dan has struck his companion at least three different times in recent months. After the most recent incident, she threatened to leave or tell the neighbors if he did it again. She tried to call her parents during one fight. Dan admits that "in her hysteria she might exaggerate the fights and make him look bad." Consequently, Dan contacted the counseling service to appease her, and because he "needs a confidant to help him deal better with the situation."

However, he thought a long time about what he was going to say to the counselor before contacting the program. His woman friend had called a shelter to get the name of a men's program— "since she had the time"—and passed the information along to him with the urging to call. What Dan really wanted was simply "some information or books that could tell me what I need to know to control my temper." As he explains, "After all, the individual has to make the changes from within. When it comes right down to it, nobody can really help you out."

Dan first struck his woman friend once several years ago while at a party. The blow cut her lip badly enough to require stitches. The woman reportedly was drinking and threw beer on him as a joke in front of his friends—"Something that was just intolerable!" Another time, Dan had been working on a school paper and asked his wife to get him a glass of orange juice. "She made some wisecrack about 'Say please' and then brought me O.J. in a soapy glass," recalls Dan. In response, he kicked the chair and threw a container of pencils at her. Most recently, Dan and his woman friend started arguing about their lost dog. The woman had left the dog out after Dan had said not to and the dog did not return. "She got all hysterical—crying and yelling—when I tried to calm her down by shaking her," recounts Dan. "I finally had to let her leave the house."

"The disagreements," according to Dan's cool analysis, are a product of the excessive demands on him. "I feel like I'm carrying twenty brief cases!" Dan, on the other hand, wants most of all to get A's in graduate school, so he spends most of his time studying. In their frequent bickering, the woman throws up the times that he has been unfaithful to her and beaten her as evidence that he does not really care. "So what am I supposed to do? I work 50 to 60 hours a week at school plus at an internship job."

Moreover, his woman friend supposedly does "dumb things" that Dan has to correct. For instance, he "carefully" gave her explicit instructions on how to use the bank card and get money, how to photocopy a paper for him, and how to maintain food stamps. In each case, "she did something wrong." (Recently, Dan took the checking account away from his woman friend, because she was "just not stable enough to handle it.") Dan, furthermore, tries to tutor the woman in some of her subjects "but without much success."

The efforts to "help" other people extend to his graduate classes, as well. In one project team to which he is assigned, Dan "ends up doing research for others in the group." He explains:

> You have to get the task done. If I didn't act, there'd be chaos and nothing would get done. You have to get down to brass tacks. You can't coddle other people or go by some round about convoluted way.

Dan goes on to talk about the annoying attitude of the others who were "there just to get the degree." The blacks were just like undergraduates, the French Canadians were hypocritical, and so on. "It just wasn't what it is supposed to be," insists Dan.

The abusive behavior is not a new thing to Dan, however. He was raised by his mother who was "stern, disciplining me regularly with broomstick beatings." His older brother would play her off against him, provoking Dan with things his mother supposedly said and vice versa, until one day Dan turned and beat his mother when she started to beat him. He also recalls kicking a young girl friend when she called him names on the playground and fist fighting with a girl friend in high school who "turned on me." Dan's opinion of women is perhaps reflected in his observation of his present relationship:

> Women seem to ask for it at times. They know you are at your limit. I've said, 'Hey, enough, let's stop.' I've tried to walk away and she keeps coming back. She calls you every name in the book and you're supposed to just take it all. There reaches a point where a man has to hold on to some of his dignity. You can't keep being put down.

Eventually, Dan was sent to an exclusive military school "in order to get the discipline and supervision I supposedly needed." His memories of this experience are not favorable either:

> The school where I lived was like living in World War II. It was like Hitler lived there. And I wasn't going to kneel down to those guys and give in. I was ready to fight, if I had to . . . .
>
> There is a little man inside that keeps you alive. Without it you would fall by the wayside. You have to struggle to survive and you can't trust others or they might do you in. Keep up your guard and avoid getting too close. That is why I am argumentative. That's what keeps you alive.

Much of Dan's relationship problems could be traced to his Machiavellian view of the world. As he summarizes this view:

> As I see the world, there are the leaders and those that are on the bottom. People have to be weeded out. If they don't fall into line they have to be put into place. It is important to have authority. Either you lead or withdraw and get out of the way. I am the kind that is able to lead and people look to me for that leadership.

Unfortunately, many of "the people" to whom Dan refers are not willing to follow as he directs.

Dan's involvement in the counseling program was shortlived. After a few confrontative sessions, Dan asserted, "I guess I am pretty set in my ways. This can't help me. If I do change at all,

I have to do it myself." He went on to explain that he felt "detached" from the group meetings; he could "see when the counselor was maneuvering me or using gimmicks." However, several months later Dan sent a letter to the program staff suggesting that he had in fact got something from his brief participation:

> Since I last saw you, I have had no outbursts. In three instances, I felt the feelings swell in me, but for some reason they seemed trite. So I ignored them. They never entered into the scheme of things. I credit my letting go, my exorcism, as being the true impetus. Our talks helped in the transition. I have let go of many things, but not in a detrimental way. The stress of school, money, and the relationship have eased. Some of their own doing . . . .

George, the fearsome delinquent

George is another small but mighty guy, but in a much different way than Dan. Rather than contemplative and detached, he is visceral and gregarious; rather than self-contained and calculating, he often appears crazed and volatile. This local delivery man has severely beaten his wife several times and sent her to the hospital for extended periods on three occasions. Prior to his own hospitalization for alcoholism, he punched her in the face, kicked her when she was down, and then proceeded to club her with a chair until she was unconscious. The woman had to be hospitalized for over six weeks after the incident.

Often times George's violence occurred when he had been drinking or using drugs, which was fairly regularly. But there were also times, George points out, that he attacked his wife without being high. During many of the beatings, he would "just black out and not even remember what happened until my wife told me the next day."

George had been committed to an alcohol and drug abuse program for several weeks as probation for his last attack. As part of his after care, he was referred to the counseling program for batterers. George, in part because of his previous participation in a variety of counseling programs, is adept at talking about himself and readily opens up to recount his background. He explains that while in the hospital he had to look at his anger, pain and violence. "I feel like scum, when I talk about it," he says. George, in fact, feels "really guilty," and this feeling has made him want "to get close to God for the first time," or so he reports.

When asked specifically why he is so violent, he says in a reflex manner, "I was brought up that way!" As George explains, "I grew up with violence and all of us kids turned out violent. My foster parents beat each other and us. And I don't care how against violence you are, if you see that all the time growing up, you are going to resort to it, too."

George was put up for adoption at 18 months, because "my mother did not want me and my father was a no good wino." He spent his younger years on a "labor farm" where he was severely beaten for not working hard enough and frequently ran away in response. Eventually, he was sent back to his mother, only to be abused further by her. Therefore, one Christmas Eve, when barely a teenager, George hitchhiked 14 hours in the snow to return to the foster family. They "brushed me off and forced me to leave." George was subsequently passed through a number of other foster homes. He threw bricks at one set of parents, threatened another with a baseball bat, and was finally sent to a boys' detention center.

There, he was pressured to perform homosexual acts and was finally raped by "the bigger kids." Nonetheless, he eventually adapted: "I'm not afraid of institutions now. They are better than being raised in a foster home, because there are no people there acting like they love you when they really don't." He notes that "he feels betrayed by the people that are supposed to have loved him."

George met his wife, formerly married and with three children, in a bar. "We didn't get off to a very good start. We knew each other mostly through sex and drugs,'' he recalls. Not long after they were married he started beating her over disagreements about handling her children. ''She would let them gulp down a gallon of milk at the table, while I'm struggling to make ends meet.'' He remembers a particularly fierce battle when she threatened to go back to school. Another fight followed her selling ''my stereo right under my nose without saying anything to me about it.''

There had been abuse over sexual relations, as well. George admits forcing his wife to have sex ''on occasion.'' ''Yes, you could call it rape if you want to, but I did it because she got stubborn.'' As he reflects on the problem, ''Maybe I'm oversexed, but when we first got married she was too. We'd go to bed two times a day, and then 'wham' she goes cold on me.''

His abuse, however, seems to have few boundaries. George admits throwing everything at her he could get his hands on and recalls even hitting the car with a crow bar so she could not drive away. After one fight, he said that if she would just hug him during a fight he would stop. The next time he got violent, she did hug him and he ''pulled two handfuls of her hair out by the roots.'' George insists that he ''just wants her to understand''—an expression that he repeats frequently. He blames her lawyer for causing the present separation and precluding his efforts to build some emotional bond. ''I am ready to hit that lawyer in court; I'm going to hurt him like he has tried to hurt me. The only way to do this is hit him so he remembers it.'' After his numerous references to hitting or being hit, George pauses to smile and chuckle.

George, while confessing to his violence and its impact, still sees his wife as playing a part in the beatings. ''She is as looney as I am, yet I'm the one in counseling. She won't go.'' He tells of trying to keep her from going to taverns at night. Supposedly, one night she ''grabbed some guy in his crotch,'' when they were both kind of drunk. George threw beer in the man's face and broke a mug over his head, before pulling his wife outside to ''slap some sense into her.'' ''She thinks I remember it and still hold it against her . . . I guess I do to some extent.''

Moreover, George's wife can be "a bitch." According to George:

> When my wife starts bitching it just doesn't stop. She bitches about the kids, bitches about not being with the kids, bitches about too much work, bitches about me not helping enough in the basement. She bitches about bitches. There's no way to stop it. You know that can really get to you.
>
> She says that her friends only have one kid or none and she has three already. And so she has to work long days keeping up with them. There's a lot of work there, I know. I try to help and get us out when I can. But you know the last time she said there is nothing to do except go to a tavern. I said you can go to a movie or bowling. And she says that's no fun. You see what I mean? It's bitch, bitch, bitch. . . .

Furthermore, his wife "keeps testing me with criticisms and complaints, probably just to see if I'll beat her again." George says that all he needs from her is a little encouragement once in a while, "that's not asking too much is it?":

> It would really help if just once she'd say "nice job." I like to fix cars and build things. That's one thing I feel I'm half good at and what do you get? Just complaints about why I didn't do it this way or that instead of "That's O.K.! I like that!" You know, just showing some kind of appreciation for you.

Part of the problem may be that George "believes you show your love by your actions," whereas his wife, according to George, "says she shows her love through her feelings."

She "can play mind games with you," George continues. "She is much smarter than I am, or acts like she is." Reportedly, she was married to a motorcycle gang member "who just left her one day for parts unknown." But she conveniently leaves some letters from him around "when she wants to eat at me."

George obviously does not feel appreciated. He claims his wife just wants him around "to take care of the kids, drive her places, or be the house watch dog." His wife retorts, however, that she doesn't want to be "possessed" by him. Nevertheless, the relationship persists even after several hospitalizations.

George's wife returned home after her recovery and a few weeks' stay with her parents. She believed that George had been rehabilitated after commitment to the alcohol and drug program, and so did George. Unfortunately, George fell back into his addictions, this time complicated with heroin use. He again was shoving his wife around when high or wanting to get high. Consequently, he was sent by his probation officer back to the detoxification program. George appears bent on destroying himself as much as others.

Al, the conscientious husband

Al, in his early fifties, is a conscientious furniture sales representative of some twenty-five years. He is the father of four children, two of whom are in college. He and his wife have had their "tense times," but only in the last few years has he ever hit anyone. He slapped his wife and gave her a black eye. He also shoved his youngest daughter into the wall and seriously hurt her head.

Peering through his thick glasses at his hands which are folded over his paunchy stomach, Al asks, "Why? Why? It just seems automatic. Something snaps and, 'wham,' I go off like a gun." He recalls recently throwing a bowl of chili at his wife and swinging at her. "She knows I don't like chili cooked with those kind of beans. But I still should not have hit her. I know that is the one thing you don't do. My father drummed that into me. You never hit a woman I mean that is about as low as you can go."

In recent years the sporadic outbursts and occasional pushings or hittings continued to intensify. Al started breaking his wife's favorite china and other possessions, as well. Finally, his wife went "on a vacation" and sent the children to stay with a relative, leaving Al to fend for himself. "I knew I needed some help but

I didn't know where to go. I thought at times maybe I was cracking up and should be sent away. But no, I was normal." Al was
sure the problem would go away with time:

> I always felt I could handle it. I didn't need doctors. I didn't
> need counselors. I could handle it. It suddenly occurred
> to me that I wasn't handling it. When my wife left me,
> I sat down and thought, "Hey, look what you've done
> to your life—to a nice family." The way I was raised—
> everything that happens is the man's responsibility. I was
> taught not to cry. You don't show your feelings . . . I
> thought I could handle anything. Actually, I could take
> care of nothing.

Al who does not drink and attends church regularly, did finally
start taking a few beers. Through a friend, whom he called ostensibly to find out what had happened to a mutual acquaintance with
a broken marriage, Al learned of the counseling program.

"I really didn't consider myself a wife beater at all," he
remarks. "I was the furthest thing from it—a conscientious husband." But when Al arrived at the counseling group, he found
"It felt good to talk about my problems." He is always on time
for the meetings, dressed still in a white shirt, and eager to review
the stressful moments at work or at home. "It is like a release
that helps me clear my head. I really notice if I miss coming."

Al grew up in a devout home where his father, who worked
two jobs, "encouraged me to take care of myself." As Al relates,
"it was important to work hard and save, if you were going to
make something of yourself. Nobody was going to do it for you."
After two years in college and a stint in the army as a quarter-
master, he came home to marry a neighborhood sweetheart and
raise a family. A job in merchandising with a relative enabled him
to comfortably support his family. But as the children grew up
and began to question his authority, he became increasingly strict.
Arguments and hurt feelings resulted.

He feels that children should obey their parents, "especially
in this time of confusion and doubt." Consequently, if his younger

daughter does not do the dishes when he tells her—right after dinner—or leaves her room messy after she was told to clean it up, "I let her know what I think about it. That's my duty. Someone has to keep them in line." Al believes that children should even be spanked if necessary: "As long as you keep it on their backside, it is acceptable. My son appreciates a good licking once in a while." The other night Al apparently swatted his son for taking the car without permission. "In the morning my son remarked, 'Gee, dad. It sure did hurt but it is better than getting thrown around the room.'" Interestingly, Al's mother, who was visiting him for a week, noted that he reprimanded the children just like his father had done in the past.

The discipline extends to his grown children, as well. As Al explains: "My oldest daughter went off and married the first thing that noticed her and now she has herself in a mess. I simply refuse to let that husband of hers in our house. He borrowed money from us supposedly for a new car and ended up spending it in some gambling deal." Al feels that America in general needs more discipline. He sees the country becoming increasingly weak because it "has lost her backbone." "We are on the brink of war because other countries have pushed us around . . . Our economy is in poor shape, because we have allowed the Japanese to undercut us in our own markets."

Al fiddles with his watch, checks the time almost out of habit, and then explains that he has "had a lot on my mind lately." There are the end of the quarter reports to be completed, a new sales representative to train ("who doesn't know what he is doing"), and his wife's mother is in poor health. "It does start to wear on a guy after a while," he sighs. Yet as the tensions mount so does Al's sense of responsibility. "Whenever my wife would empty her basket of problems, I felt I had to fix them all."

Al admits that he only has really one outlet. He does not go out that much except to business club meetings and seldom talks to other men, relatives or neighbors about himself. He simply tinkers around the house, occasionally building a lamp or two, but with great care. As he reflects on his style:

I admit that I am a perfectionist. If you're going to do something you might as well do it right. Why have the bricks out of line or a nail bent if you, with a little more effort, can do it right? I know my wife or children offer to help me sometimes, but it isn't always worth it because I'm so demanding. I realize I should be a little more patient but it is hard.

Al's life is otherwise routine. "It is a matter of knowing what to do and simply going out there and doing it. But the increasing red tape for small businesses makes it more and more difficult to keep on top of your work."

As he reexamines his abusive incidents, Al recalls that he "had just had it." When asked why he did not do something about his feelings before they turned to violence, he explains, "I should not have to tell people that I'm fed up. They should have enough sense to know that they are out of line." Interestingly, he does not talk specifically of his wife without prodding. Rather than implicate her in the abuse, he degrades her housemaker role:

I give her all sorts of things, too much in fact. I let her decorate the house, the way she wanted and gave her the money she needed. I was giving, giving, and she was fretting about little things.

Al's wife did return after her few weeks vacation and he continued to attend meetings regularly for over a year. As he spent more and more time at the program meetings, he moved beyond descriptions of his incidents and talked freely of his feelings. "It is funny. You never talk about how you feel with the people you work with. . . .They'd laugh at you if they heard the way we are talking here."

Al has become one of the program "converts," as he describes himself. "All I know is that coming to the meetings has changed me. I have begun to see myself more as an individual, instead of the way I thought I was supposed to be. I don't have to do everything for everybody. I start by making sure I have my own tent in order.'' Al in his enthusiasm went on to do interviews for the media on the problem of wife abuse and started organizing other men to meet in groups and take action.

The Issue of Control

As mentioned at the outset of this chapter, the men who batter might be characterized as desperate individuals who control their wives as a means of maintaining some sense of self-esteem, authority, and privilege. When the men are prompted to interpret their violence, they most often see the incident in isolation, that is, independent of social forces or norms. Once they do admit to the violence, they at least share the blame with their spouse or cohabitant. Some even lapse into a kind of self-pity that puts all of the blame on the women, as the profiles suggest. Seldom are the men able to empathize with the women's state of fear and terror at their husband's volatility. The men appear to have difficulty enough discovering their own feelings, let alone those of their victims.

In the course of group discussions, many men do begin to relate their violence to the violence they experienced in their family of origin. This realization, however, often amounts to a shift of the blame and an awakened resentment towards one's parents. Some of these men do begin to acknowledge the toll that their work has on their private lives. However financially rewarding, their work leaves all but a few regimented, stressed, and disillusioned. In the hierarchical business world, one's ability as a family provider is minimal; it is beating another competitor that lifts one higher in the power structure. Only a few manage to win big at this game. Consequently, men are left to exercise their prowess in the one domain left to them—their home. Not coincidently, the public in a capitalist society fights hard to keep the family domain free of government interference. It is after all the last sanctuary—or ''castle''—for many men in an overbearing corporate society.

Nevertheless, this larger sociological analysis barely surfaces regardless of the implications in one's immediate experience. The issue of control, which most of the profiled men do begin to identify in their assessments of their abuse, may, however, provide a link between the personal and sociological domains of explanation. The following consideration of control and abuse attempts to clarify this connection so often slighted in prevailing theory and practice.

Toward a Conceptual Framework

Several researchers have begun to chart the interrelation of the psychological and sociological workings that form the batterer. At the center of their considerations is how this sense of control is readily translated into violence. Gelles (1983:157), for instance, forwards an exchange/social control theory which basically asserts that "people hit and abuse other family members because they can." There are few sanctions against hitting women and many gains. If a man's status is threatened by hitting a woman, he can conveniently excuse himself with disclaimers like "I was drunk." The violence, in this light, appears more instrumental; that is, it is a means to maintaining one's self-interest.

Ball-Rokeach (1980) suggests that the conflict is more internally motivated. The conflict is over scarce resources arising from "asymmetrical social relations" and is essentially an effort to influence the distribution of these "scarce resources by the threat of exertion and physical force" (Ball-Rokeach, 1980:46). More simply, the abuse is goal-oriented and rational. Rather than inflicting harm for its own sake, men abuse women to get something they want.

Researchers, nevertheless, cannot overlook the emotional realm behind wife abuse, according to Berkowitz (1983). In his interviews with violent criminals, Berkowitz (1979) found that 40% of the men actually wanted to hurt their victim, but their desire to inflict pain was related to some unpleasant feelings. In sum, adversive events instigate aggression and a desire to escape or avoid the unpleasant. As Berkowitz (1983:174) concludes:

> I contend that all aversive events, whether frustrations, deprivations, noxious stimuli, or environmental stresses, produce an instigation to be aggressive as well as a desire to escape or avoid the unpleasant situation.

The violent act is partly, therefore, involuntary or impulsive. The violence may be "expressive" (simply a release of anger), as well as instrumental (debilitating the perceived source of the adversity).

Dutton et al. (1982, 1984) perhaps best model the relations of the sociological and psychological dynamics in their application of Zimbardo's cognitive conception of "deindividuated violence" to wife abuse (see Table 3-2). Similar to the exchange/social control theory of Gelles, normative control over behavior breaks down. As Berkowitz' notion of aggression suggests, some psychological arousal results. (Dutton suggests, furthermore, that some batterers are motivated by a need to actually produce conflict-based arousal, if they do not receive some.) Rather than unremitting impulsiveness, however, there is a cognitive dimension involved. The men label their arousal as anger, anxiety or some other emotion. Because of male socialization, the men most often label their arousal as anger and have sanctions and reinforcements to express that anger as violence. They, too, are more likely to perceive initial events as a threat because of the power imbalances that they so desperately maintain.

In Dutton's scheme, the participating event must be perceived as threatening; the perception instigates a psychological arousal; the arousal is then labeled as anger; the anger leads to consequential violent action. This conception of deindividuated violence appears to favor the interpretation that male violence is largely unprovoked. The implication is that research should consider wife abuse less as some unified phenomenon of men and women. Instead, it should devote more to investigating the male cognitive and emotional process instigated and maintained by male socialization and social privilege.

Table 3-2: A Cognitive Model of Deindividuated Violence

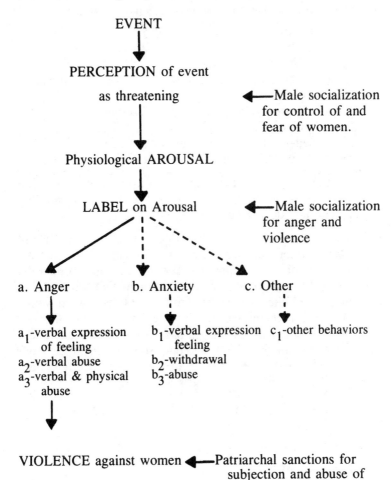

EVENT

PERCEPTION of event
as threatening ◀——Male socialization
for control of and
fear of women.

Physiological AROUSAL

LABEL on Arousal ◀——Male socialization
for anger and
violence

a. Anger   b. Anxiety   c. Other

a_1-verbal expression b_1-verbal expression c_1-other behaviors
of feeling   feeling
a_2-verbal abuse b_2-withdrawal
a_3-verbal & physical b_3-abuse
abuse

VIOLENCE against women ◀——Patriarchal sanctions for
subjection and abuse of
women

From: Donald Dutton, "An Ecological Nested Theory," in P. Caplan, ed., *Feminist Psychology in Transition* Montreal: Eden Press, 1984.

How an individual man evolves from an occasionally aggressive husband to a chronic batterer is suggested in Bern's (1982) conception of an "on-going interactional process" in which the batterer, according to labeling theory, defines himself as one who must use violence in the relationship. As Bern (1982:24) points out:

> The man believes that he must use violence to maintain power; his spouse reacts toward him as a violent person; he does release hostile impulses, which serves to reinforce the behavior; and his power in the relationship is maintained—a strong reinforcer for a man who is often struggling with feelings of inadequacy.

Most men, nevertheless, experience many of the same feelings of low self-esteem, desire for control, and anger toward their wives. Yet they do not become violent.

Why some men let their frustrations well-up in rage and abuse, and others do not, remains, of course, a complex question and difficult to predict (see Monahan, 1981). There is no doubt that some have been more systematically taught that violence is a suitable outlet. Others have turned their hostilities toward women inward, inflicting themselves with physical duress. Still others express their hostility by exerting a passive-aggressive smugness, rather than become physically violent. Some release their anger through golf, bowling, or softball; drown it successfully in beer; or redirect it toward their business adversaries.

In any case, the issue of control persists. It is a matter that warrants further elaboration and ultimately a response.

The Elements of Control

How does this sense of control manifest itself? It is more than just the domination of others but rather includes three interrelated elements, as the profiles suggest. This sense of control is manifested in: 1) an excessive regulation of one's own behavior and feelings; 2) an overbearing responsibility for others; 3) a privilege to be in authority. This ideal of control, however, is either counter-productive or impossible to attain.

The first element of the penchant for control is a *constraining sense of self-control*. The men in the profiles are adamant about being in-charge of their own behavior. For instance, at the first phone contact, the majority of men explain that they did not know why they were calling. They could handle the problem themselves; a friend or their spouse had made them call for help. This defensiveness reflects the familiar masculine conception of self-control. A man is to be rational, analytical, and unemotional. He is ultimately the master of his own destiny, the one who has to make the changes.

There are those, too, who have an even more sophisticated defense against the threat of losing control to therapists. The more educated are keenly analytical to the point that they emotionally suspend themselves from a discussion and objectively evaluate all the "games" that are being played on them. This sort of control, of course, supersedes their personal involvement in the group dynamics. It takes some forthright confrontation to bring these men into genuine participation—confrontation that risks driving them away from the program completely.

Self-containment is especially apparent in the men's repression of emotion, as discussed in Chapter 2. The men who batter do not have the experience or facility to communicate feelings that begin to swell up inside. The inability to sort through these feelings leaves the men trapped. To let out the tensions, stress, fear, and anger is to risk an explosion that their self-image cannot handle. They might just lose control if they try to deal with the volatile material churning inside. Consequently, they hold it in.

As the men increasingly suppress their emotions, an emotional numbness begins to set in. Although many emotions are present, they become so layered over with denial and avoidance that they are not consciously present. The undercurrent of emotions often causes periods of inexplicable depressions. But these moods, too, are covered over, if not with more avoidance, then with alcohol, drugs, and sex. The men in a sense become "unfeeling," losing perhaps love for their spouse, as well. The batterers, then, are so "in control" but detached from their emotions that they are oblivious to the mounting rage until it erupts in violence.

A second element of control is an *overbearing sense of responsibility for others*. As time-honored providers, the men feel accountable especially for their family's well-being and status. The behavior, attitude, and even appearance of their children, wives, relatives, and friends in turn reflects on them. Therefore, they speak not only of controlling themselves, but also of controlling the demeanor of others in order to protect their reputation. If severe problems do arise, it is consequently easy to blame the family members and absolve oneself.

Batterers in one group session, spontaneously told of their constant mental planning, organizing and regulating of finances, relationships, and activities. One batterer even mentioned lying in bed at night planning for his family's summer vacation. It was February at the time! The men get mad when the kitchen does not get cleaned as expected, their plans for the weekend are interrupted, the kids obey the mother instead of them. In sum, they try to control others behavior in the same rigid manner reflected in their own behavior patterns. This effort is compounded by the objectification that emerges as men control and repress their feelings. They begin to relate more and more to other beings as objects, since they themselves are out of touch with feelings.

A third manifestation of control is the male *expectation of privilege*—a kind of control of status and social rewards. The men feel that they deserve some privileges in return for maintaining order; that is, they expect some concessions, respect, and rewards for their job of managing themselves and others. If a man should fly-off-the-handle now and then, he should not be made to feel guilty or be accused. After all, he has a difficult role to bear as controller, manager, and provider, or so the batterer's logic goes.

Consequently, one of the biggest challenges is getting men to accept responsibility for their violence. All sorts of denials arise, but most suggest that they have to "keep their woman" in line. They consider women to be at least accomplices in the violence. Their mothers, wives, daughters, and old girl friends, in the batterer's view, "set them up." These clients view women as receiving help from the community, while the men themselves receive little. Community's are often hesitant to support a men's program, considering the needs of abused women or the stigma associated with "wife beaters." As one abuser explained:

> That's the problem. These women want everything. There's nothing for the men. We are the one's that end up getting dumped on. How much is a person supposed to take? We deserve some respect too, you know!

The Techniques of Control

Wife beating is often defined as the assaultive behavior by a more powerful mate on the less powerful mate (Gangely, 1981). However, this control of another can take a variety of forms that go beyond our conventional sense of "wife beating." Walker (1979:71-184) discusses a typology of battering techniques that includes the physical abuse (with which we are most familiar), sexual battering, psychological battering, and destruction of property (see Table 3-3).

Sexual abuse is, for instance, a widespread form of abuse, yet one less discernible and less likely to be considered a technique of control. Contrary to conventional wisdom, rape of strangers or spouses has been diagnosed as a means to feel powerful, rather than a lust for sexual gratification (Groth, 1979). Russell (1982) estimates that one in seven women in the United States is raped by her husband sometime during their relationship and one in four is forced into some kind of unwanted sexual experience. She also documents the association of sexual abuse with other forms of wife abuse. She indicates that there may be a continuum of violence used against wives—that is, other forms of abuse are used to force women into more severe forms of sexual abuse (see also Finkelhor and Yllo, 1982).

Table 3-3: Definitions of Battering

Wife battering is defined as *the assaultive behavior by the more powerful mate on the less powerful mate in the context of an intimate relationship*. Battering may be defined as the assaultive behavior between adult intimates and categorized in four forms: 1) Physical battering, 2) Sexual battering, 3) Psychological battering, and 4) Destruction of property and pets. These are not totally separate due to some obvious overlap.

Physical battering includes all aggressive behavior done by the offender to the victim's body. Pushing, pinching, spitting, kicking, pulling hair, hitting, punching, choking, burning, clubbing, stabbing, throwing acid or boiling water, shooting, etc.

Sexual battering includes physical attacks on the victim's breasts/genitals or forced sexual activity accompanied by either battering or threat of physical battery. Examples include forcing sexual activity after a beating, requiring performance of sexual activities under threat of battery, or forcing unwanted sexual activities.

Psychological battering is carried out with psychological weapons rather than physical attack. 1) Threats, such as threatening suicide, threatening violence against a mate or others, threatening to take the children away, etc. 2) Forcing the victim to do degrading things such as eat cigarette butts, lick the kitchen floor, etc. 3) Controlling the victim's activities such as sleeping and eating habits, social relationships, access to money, etc. 4) Constant attacks on a mate's self esteem by verbal abuse. 5) Doing things to intentionally frighten the victim such as speeding through traffic or playing with weapons.

Psychological battering takes place in a relationship where there has been at least one episode of physical battering. The power of psychological battering comes from the violence that has already occurred.

Destruction of property and pets, unlike physical or sexual battering, takes place without actually attacking or ever touching the victim's body. However this is still considered an assault on the victim. The destruction is not random, it is the victim's favorite china thrown against the wall, or her gift torn up in front of her, or her pet cat strangled. Sometimes a batterer destroys his own treasured objects, then blames his mate for causing their ruin. Or, to make a point, he throws an object at his mate just missing her head. The victim never knows when assaults on property will turn into physical assaults, and the destruction of property often has the same psychological effect on the victim as a physical attack.

Battering does not fall onto a continuum, ranging from least to most serious. *All types of battering are considered serious*. The reality is that shoving can be as or more dangerous than punching when evaluted in terms of the potential injury to the victim.

Whether battering is physical, sexual, psychological, or destruction of pet/property, all forms have certain characteristics in common: 1) All are done without concern for the physical or mental well being of the victim. 2) All forms are done to show control and dominance, to attempt to gain control in a situation in which the batterer feels insecure, anxious or helpless. 3) Regardless of the form which occurs, usually the incidents of battering are recurrent, often escalating in severity and frequency unless the batterer makes necessary changes in behavior.

From: Men for Non-Violence, Ft. Wayne, IN; adopted from Anne Ganley, *Court Mandated Counseling for Men Who Batter*. Center for Women's Policy Studies, Washington, D.C., 1981, pp. 8-16.

Men, furthermore, destroy favorite possessions or pets of their spouse as a way to coerce and control them. Or, they may withhold money or access to the car to isolate and intimidate their wives. The majority of abusers, in fact, use a constellation of abusive techniques that include abuse against children and often against relatives and acquaintances (Fagan et al., 1983).

Even in less than violent relationships, a form of psychological battering persists once there has been one violent episode. A wife, even though she is not subsequently "touched," is likely to remain in terror. She waits in frightened anticipation of the next incident.

In most cases, the violence can come without warning or provocation, so the woman has to be ever on guard. In fact, it is not uncommon for battered women to report keeping themselves awake every night until their husbands fall asleep so that they will not be assaulted in their sleep when they can offer no defense. Therefore, it is important to recognize that even though an abuser may report that he has relinquished his control—that is, he has not hit his wife recently,—his spouse most likely is still subjected by the terror of an unexpected incident.

Moreover, the relationship may amount to a kind of brainwashing with the husband convincing the wife she is hysterical or guilty of the suffering (Walker, 1979). Some researchers have equated the experience to that of a prisoner of war who under the subjection of intermittent punishment actually begins to identify with his or her oppressor (Dutton and Painter, 1981).

Implications for Treatment

The control issue has mediating implications for the debate over treatment. Although there is evidence of mutual aggression between partners (associated in Chapter 2 with the social learning theory), wife abuse can be subsumed by the notion that the batterers are over conforming to a stereotypic image of "men as dominant" (associated with the sociopolitical theory).

The discussion of the control issue suggests that the most immediate concern to battering men is control of their wives' verbal aggression and their own explosive anger. But it is clear from the profiles that the men also need to unlearn their overbearing sense of rigidity, domination, and control that they associate with manhood. It is this sense of control that instigates much of a wife's apparent antagonism. It is a vestige of patriarchal power that becomes increasingly inappropriate and self-destructive. In most of the profiles, as the batterers became "feminized," however slightly, their relationships improved and their violence subsided. As they began to share decisions, responsibility, and authority and nurture their own individuality, they in fact changed and were able to change others.

The issue of control has implications for the kind of program that will best suit men who batter. Individuals with such a tenuous sense of control perceive directive clinical treatment as further aggravation. Submitting to professional psychologists or mental health workers implies, as discussed in Chapter 1, a loss of independence, self-reliance, and authority. The counselor appears as an expert telling the abuser what to do—a fact that can lead to a competitive duel between client and therapist.

A self-help format gives a batterer some sense of control in his "treatment" by placing more of the responsibility for change on the abuser; therefore, it may be less threatening to the abuser, as mentioned in Chapter 1. Moreover, the self-help type of program can offer men who batter an experience of genuine sharing through the opportunity of discussing their problems with others who are in a similar situation. In this way, the process of change goes beyond the individual to an identification with a group. This involvement usually exposes emotions that need to be soothed and relationships that beg for reconciliation. However, it does not always bring to the surface the circumstances that established a particular individual's predisposition for violence or the perpetuation of it. Thus, there is a need for a trained supervisor to help guide the group members toward confronting the roots of their controlling behaviors. This is the subject of the following chapters.

4

Hotline to Group
Participation

The notion of self-help groups often raises an image of a loosely formed network of individuals with a problem in common. The leadership usually emerges from the group itself, and plans and decisions are made on an ad hoc basis. Consequently, many self-help efforts that follow this open format are short-lived and occasionally disorganized.

As discussed in Chapter 1, there are, however, organizational considerations that can make a self-help group more enduring and more effective. In establishing a successful program for men, several fundamental aspects must be fully developed, according to the trends apparent in the existing men's programs.

A national survey of the existing men's services (Roberts, 1982) confirms diversity in organizational structure but indicates some prevalent features that suggest a trend in program format. The majority of the services maintain a hotline or crisis counseling phone service, one salaried counselor or trained facilitator, and a group counseling component. Most draw on a meager budget solicited from local donations and modest fees to meet operating expenses. An array of volunteer support, however, keeps most programs going. The most frequently mentioned problems cited by the services are those related to the batterer's lack of motivation, in particular their high dropout rates.

This chapter presents a program format that reflects these prevailing features and addresses the issue of control discussed in the previous chapter. It also identifies the most pressing problems encountered in the counseling process and how to meet them. To this end, the chapter considers the following aspects of program development: obtaining a facility or central meeting place, training and recruiting staff, and instituting a mechanisms for receiving and working with clients.

The Facility

Finding and arranging for a meeting place is the first consideration any potential program must face. Many batterers are tremendously reluctant to contact a counseling program; therefore, the more convenient to phone and visit, the more likely the program is to be patronized. At least the men will have a few less excuses for not attending if the program is readily accessible. A slick downtown office complete with receptionist is often too remote in location and too professional in ambiance for most batterers seeking such a program. At the same time, too casual an atmosphere or counterculture appearance is likely to offend the abuser's extreme sense of masculinity fixed on control and traditional values. The program's facility, therefore, should appear more like a comfortable living room rather than a professional building.

Of course, some preliminary groundwork needs to be laid in acquiring and establishing such a facility. As discussed in Chapter 1, a cooperative agreement needs to be made with the state and local women's groups working with battered wives. Staff members also need to visit local social services, police, and churches to explain in detail the proposed program. Such visits provide an opportunity to enlist cooperation and support which could be critical to the success of a new program. In short, there are likely to be questions and even objections to the idea of "violent" men gathering to talk about their problems. Consequently, the staff or supporters of the program must be prepared to explain the rationale and nature of the batterers' program.

The prominent location of many program facilities raises an essential issue about the danger which potentially violent clients pose to the community. Even though 80% of the men who batter have a single target for their violence—their wives (Walker, 1979:24), the program or organization should offer a decisive policy on violence which can communicate some reassurances to the surrounding community. The program, therefore, should establish its opposition to violence but also its preparedness to prevent violence on the premises.

A clear policy statement on violence also gives new staff, in particular, a means to anticipate the possibility of a violent outburst in the rare event that one should occur. Some of the issues to be considered might include: How can staff avoid inciting or allowing a violent event to occur in their offices? What support or back-up is available if a client is uncontrollable or unruly? What are the staff's responsibilities if a client wishes them to visit him at home? What recourse should staff members take if caught in a fight between husband and wife? (See Table 4-1.) Few existing programs report any problems of this nature. However, many urge their staff to be alert given the alcohol and drug abuse of many of their clients.

The Staff

However, the success of programs for men who batter is not so much contingent on its facilities or credentials, as it is on the quality of its workers. A second consideration, then, is the commitment and effectiveness of the staff. The counseling can commence with one counselor and a few interested abusers, although, as suggested, a substantial amount of community support before starting is vital. The more successful programs recommend, nevertheless, that two trained counselors be on hand for a group of six to ten men who batter.

Table 4-1: Working With Potentially Violent Clients

Introduction: Men's programs in general report few outburst of violence or potential danger from clients. However, it is important that the staff consider the possibility of encountering violence and be prepared to confront it or prevent it. The staff needs to be especially alert if called to a client's home or a shelter. Here are some strategies for working with potentially violent clients as outlined by experienced social workers:

1. Find out if there is an agency or organization policy in regard to violence and, if not, press for one.

2. Set up a communication system with co-workers. We should discuss cases so we have input about potentially violent clients from workers who carried these cases previously. We need to share information constantly.

3. Be aware of territoriality . . . we should think carefully about when to insist on an office visit, when it is necessary to make a home visit, when to take someone with us, and whom we should take—co-worker or sheriff.

4. Knowledge of cultural issues can be lifesaving as well as useful for more sensitive handling of charged situations. Male workers should be aware of the impact of making home visits on housewives or if the husbands would consider the visits compromising situations.

5. During home visits, we should position ourselves near the door at all times. In domestic conflict situations, we should try to keep the contestants at a distance but not by getting in the middle. Seasoned policemen often use the verbal ploy "Would you get me a glass of water?" We can develop other ways to initiate cooling off periods.

6. We should know what our backup is or how to create it. Do we have the telephone numbers of police and fire departments taped to our phone? When our intuition tells us to, do we alert the sheriff that we are going to make house calls in a lonely area? Do we know first aid? CPR? How to get an ambulance? Do we have a flashlight and first-aid kit in our car?

7. How do we present ourselves? This is the key to safety. If we are running scared and showing it or masking it with false bravado, we could become a target.

8. Is the climate of our office conducive to frustration because of long waiting periods, poor ventilation, uncomfortable chairs, and noise? Or are there courteous clerks, coffee, toys for the children, reading materials, and pleasant surroundings?

From: Stephen Kaplan and Eugenia Wheeler, "Survival Skills for Working With Potentially Violent Clients," *Social Casework*, 1983, pp. 345-346.

The lead counselor can structure and direct the group's weekly discussion session. This person might open with introductory "check-ins," pinpoint trouble spots and initiate exercises. The second counselor assists by keeping track of the time, asking for clarification or focus, and encouraging the non-talkers to speak. Also, the counseling team can offer an important example of cooperation, rather than competition, through their interaction before the group. The two counselors, moreover, can enhance their counseling with feedback during the meeting and debriefing after it.

The group leaders do not need intensive training in counseling techniques, although some group counseling skills are required. What is most needed by the leaders is a feeling for the nature of wife abuse. Traditional counseling methods can lead a well intentioned counselor to reduce the social dimensions of abuse to a psychological level. Also, counseling techniques can be used unconsciously to distance the counselor from topics that relate to him personally. It is questionable, for instance, that a counselor can be as effective helping another man face his anger when he harbors many hostilities of his own.

Interestingly, many studies indicate that psychotherapy itself may not be a significant factor in changing behavior (see Zilbergeld, 1983). What is crucial is not the technique, but the relationship that develops between the counselor and counseled. This is instructive particularly in helping men who batter, because they are often extremely suspicious of counseling and need, most of all, to experience a relationship which can break down their social isolation. They need some one with whom to talk, to feel, and to identify. They need to experience a substantial relationship which serves as a model for dealing with other people, especially those in their family.

The group leaders, therefore, are best able to listen and respond if they have consciously worked through the gut issues of wife abuse themselves (see Lloyd et al., 1983). This can come, of course, through participating in group sessions with battering men and battered women, or through intensive training designed to raise the emotional dimensions of the problem—namely, the prospective counselor's response to stress, anger, violence, control and power in his own life. In particular, the staff need to evaluate their own relationship with women and their image of women. Besides confronting these issues head on, many useful training films, manuals, and books can provide a catalyst in this regard. (See Table 4-2 for an inventory of important questions to help staff members develop needed self-awareness; also, consult the Appendix for resources dealing with sex roles and wife abuse which can develop an appreciation of the issues.)

As suggested in Chapter 2, men in general are potential abusers. Therefore, in the momentum of group counseling, male counselors are liable to unconsciously reinforce men who batter. However, as the counselors become alert to their own biases, they are less likely to deflect or sympathize with those which others raise about themselves. Moreover, as they root out their own shortcomings, they become better role models for other men.

In the process of asking questions of themselves and making changes in their own behavior, they will appear more as fellow-travelers than as advice-givers. Also, counselors will be more likely to disclose their struggles and accomplishments; a process which may prompt other men to do the same.

Working With Clients

The most important aspect of any program, without a doubt, is the service to the "clients" themselves. A program's contact with men who batter is especially crucial since most men, as explained, are elusive and resistant to help. Seeking and receiving help may, as has been suggested, go against the nature of men who batter. The proper contact and introduction, therefore, is an important consideration in working with the batterer and must be carefully considered. Formation of the group and addressing the problems that arise in them is the next most important area of concern.

Table 4-2: Counselor Inventory

Instructions: This collection of questions serves as a guide for reflection to prospective counselors. It is important that male counselors be conscious of their own tendencies in these areas and be reevaluating them as they move into positions of leadership. The questions can be responded to privately in a journal or in the course of a group discussion among other counselors or trainees.

1. **Violence**

   How much and what kind of violence did you experience growing up? In what ways are you violent today? What makes you angry and how do you handle your anger? In what instance might violence be justifiable? What situations are particularly stressful for you? How do you respond to them? Do you have any predictable reaction to violence, anger, or stress? Do you ever use alcohol or drugs when you are upset?

2. **Power**

   Are you a particularly ambitious person? What is "success" to you and how do you strive to attain it? Can you note the sorts of power you have acquired and whom it affects? Do you feel especially good when you are in charge of other people?

3. **Self-Control**

   Do you feel particularly good when you accomplish a difficult task all by yourself? Are you hesitant to rely on other people or open up to them? When was the last time you asked someone specifically for help? What problems do you prefer to keep to yourself? Is it important to you that certain things be done on time and in a certain way? How do you feel when they are not and what do you do? When did you last feel really joyful, sad, inspired, hurt, intimate, alone?

4. **Women**

   What to you is the ideal woman? How important a factor is physique in your judgment of a woman? To what extent do you talk to women about your ambitions, your accomplishments, your fears, your shortcomings? How often does sex cross your mind when you are conversing with a woman? What have you done recently to help your wife, woman friend, or female co-worker? When have you agreed with or complimented a woman in order to appease her and avoid argument?

5. **Sex**

   Do you consider your sex life to be "normal?" Why or why not? Have you ever forced a woman to have sex with you against her will? How frequently do you think of doing so? How would you react if your wife or lover were raped? Have you ever thought that you might be a homosexual? What did you do about it? How would you act toward a friend who disclosed that he is homosexual?

The Initial Phone Contact

Most newcomers to a program contact the organization through some form of hotline service (see Table 4-3). The hotline may simply be an office phone at the YMCA which forwards messages to a volunteer's place of work or home. It may also be a professional answering service that automatically "peeps" an on-duty counselor. Most often, a man's first call is for information rather than crisis counseling. The counselor, in response, can assert that participation in the program represents an opportunity for the batterer to discuss his problems with other men like himself, and that such an effort has helped many men to stop their violent behavior. Typically behind this initial inquiry there is, nevertheless, a recent incident of fear that needs to be discerned and addressed.

The most important objective, however, is to get the caller to come to the program's office for an introductory interview. The caller might simply be told that, in an interview, he can find out more about the program and its appropriateness for him. In the process, it is essential to establish a mutually convenient meeting time for the introductory interview. Despite such initial efforts it has been determined that as many as 25% of the callers may not show.

The Introductory Interview

The introductory interview is crucial (see Table 4-4). During the one hour meeting, the abuser must first be sufficiently confronted to realize the extent and consequence of his violence as well as the responsibility that he has in stopping it. However, if he is challenged to the point of feeling accused or threatened, he is likely to never return. Many programs use some sort of questionnaire on violence to access the abuser's exposure to and involvement in violent behavior (see Table 4-5 and 4-6). After the man has answered each specific question, the composite of answers can be used to instruct him in the nature and extent of his violence. In this way, the counselor can begin to move the man toward acknowledging that he has a problem of violence and that this problem is not as simple as "How do I get my wife back?"

Table 4-3: Answering the Hotline

Hotline counselors or volunteers should consider the following steps when responding to a call from a man who batters.

- Identify the program and your first name.

- Respond to the caller's initial inquiries.

- Explain briefly the nature of the program and its counseling.

- Assure the caller that he can change but it takes work and involvement in a program.

- Add that he is not alone and can meet men in similar situations in the program.

- Inquire about his wife's and children's condition, whereabouts, and safety.

- Insist that the man stop harassing his woman friend immediately or he will only push her further away.

- Ask how he is feeling at the moment and inquire about his condition.

- Make an appointment for an introductory interview, reaffirming the time and directions to the program office.

- Congratulate the man for calling—it is a difficult step to take!

Adapted from: "Telephone Answering Tips," *Raven*, St. Louis, MO.

Table 4-4: Outline for Introductory Interview

The following are procedures to consider in conducting the crucial introductory interview with a man who batters.

1. Conduct *Violent Behavior Inventory* (see Table 4-5).

2. Investigate *safety of wife and children*
   Appraise man of legal consequences to behavior.
   Request permission to phone shelter or wife to verify safety.

3. Have men recount most *recent violent incident.*
   Inquire of his feelings at points in the account.
   Note connection of preceding events and the violent act.
   Ask about physical sensations that may serve as clues to impending abuse.

4. Obtain *background information.*
   Reasons for attending program and expectations.
   Marital history and the nature of present relationship.
   Parental relationship, past and present.
   Work conditions.
   Extent of alcohol and drug use.
   Military and prison history.
   Educational level and religious training.
   Medical problems and medications.
   Other counseling experiences.
   Questions or comments from the man.

5. Establish a *contractual agreement.*
   Require attendance of set number of meetings.
   Explain terms of confidentiality and group rules (see Table 4-7).
   Set forth some short term objectives.
   Decide on fee and payment policy.
   Make assignment to a group.

6. Assess the *present condition* of the man and make appropriate referrals.

Table 4-5: Violent Behavior Inventory

Instructions: (to be read aloud by interviewer)
I am going to read a list of things you may or may not have done when you and your spouse/partner had a dispute or at any other time. These are ways of being violent that people in our program report. Please tell me how often you did each one. (These questions refer to the client's present relationship.)

1	2	3	4	prior to 6	previous 6
Never	Once or Twice	Sometimes	A lot	mo. ago	months

A. Not Physically Violent
  1. Discussed issue calmly ____ ____
  2. Sulked, refused to talk, withdrew affection or sex to punish ____ ____
  3. Stomped out in order to punish ____ ____
  4. Screamed, insulted or swore at the other ____ ____
  5. Verbally pressured other to have sex ____ ____
  6. Threatened to leave the marriage or relationship ____ ____
  7. Threatened punishment other than physical (e.g., withholding money, taking away children, having an affair) ____ ____

B. Indirect Threats of Violence
  1. Threatened to hit or throw something at the other ____ ____
  2. Intentionally interrupted the other's sleeping, or other's eating ____ ____

C. Direct Threats of Violence
  1. Threatened to hit or throw something at the other ____ ____
  2. Threw, hit, or kicked something ____ ____
  3. Drove recklessly to frighten the other ____ ____
  4. Directed anger at or threatened the children ____ ____
  5. Directed anger at or threatened the pets ____ ____

D. Direct Violence
  1. Threw something at the other ____ ____
  2. Pushed, carried, restrained, grabbed, shoved, wrestled the other ____ ____
  3. Slapped or spanked the other ____ ____
  4. Bit or scratched the other ____ ____
  5. Threw the other bodily ____ ____

1 Never	2 Once or Twice	3 Sometimes	4 A lot	prior to 6 mo. ago	previous 6 months

E. Severe Violence

1. Choked or strangled the other   _____   _____
2. Physically forced sex on the other   _____   _____
3. Punched or kicked the other   _____   _____
4. Burned the other   _____   _____
5. Kicked or punched the other in the
   stomach when pregnant   _____   _____
6. Beat the other unconscious   _____   _____
7. Threatened with knife, gun or other
   weapon   _____   _____
8. Used any weapon against the other   _____   _____

From: Domestic Abuse Project, Minneapolis, MN.

A second objective of the interview is to establish the safety of the women or children affected and the abuser's relationship to them. If the batterer agrees, it may be wise to establish phone contact with the battered woman to assure her safety and verify the man's initial accounts. (In fact, many programs like RAVEN require a security check before accepting a man into a group.) In this regard, it may be useful to appraise the man of the criminal aspects of his behavior, as well as the "orders of protection" that may be used against him. This information can serve as an important motivator when leverage is needed.

Third, one way to begin to help the abuser is to have him recount the most recent incident of violence. The abuser is usually perplexed, at this point, about his behavior and its motivations. "Why do I do it? Why? Why? It just seems to happen!" is a common claim. By having him tell his story, the counselor can interject emphasis, encourage him to elaborate, and begin to note

Table 4-6: CRA Abuse Index

Directions: For each question, indicate the number from the scale below (0-3) that best describes your relationship with your wife or lover.

Frequently	Sometimes	Rarely	Never
3	2	1	0

Points

_____ 1. Do you continually monitor your wife's time and make her account for every minute (when she runs errands, visits friends, commutes to work, etc.)?

_____ 2. Do you ever accuse her of having affairs with other men or act suspicious of her?

_____ 3. Are you ever rude to your wife's friends?

_____ 4. Do you ever discourage her from starting friendships with other women?

_____ 5. Are you ever critical of things such as her cooking, her clothes or her appearance?

_____ 6. Do you demand a strict account of how your wife spends money?

_____ 7. Do your moods change radically, from very calm to very angry, or vice versa?

_____ 8. Are you disturbed by your wife's working or by the thought of her working?

_____ 9. Do you become angry more easily when you drink?

_____ 10. Do you pressure your wife for sex much more often than she likes?

_____ 11. Do you become angry if your wife does not want to go along with your requests for sex?

_____ 12. Do you and your wife quarrel much over financial matters?

_____ 13. Do you quarrel much about having children or raising them?

_____ 14. Do you ever strike your wife with your hands or feet (slap, punch, kick, etc.)?

_____ 15. Do you ever strike her with an object?

_____ 16. Do you ever threaten her with an object or weapon?

_____   17. Have you ever threatened to kill either her or yourself?

_____   18. Do you ever give your wife visible injuries (such as welts, bruises, cuts, etc.)?

_____   19. Has your wife ever had to treat any injuries from your violence with first aid?

_____   20. Has she ever had to seek professional aid for any injury at a medical clinic, doctors office, or hospital emergency room?

_____   21. Do you ever hurt your wife sexually or make her have intercourse against her will?

_____   22. Are you ever violent toward children?

_____   23. Are you ever violent toward other people outside your home and family?

_____   24. Do you ever throw objects or break things when you are angry?

_____   25. Have you ever been in trouble with the police?

_____   26. Has your wife ever called the police or tried to call them because she felt she or members of your family were in danger?

_____   Total

To score responses simply add up the points for each question. This sum is your Abuse Index Score. To get some idea of how abusive your relationship is, compare your Index Score with the following chart:

120-92 Dangerously abusive
 91-35 Seriously abusive
 34-13 Moderately abusive
 12-0 Nonabusive

If at all possible, your wife should also complete a CRA Abuse Index form. The differences in the results should be discussed with the program counselor. Do you grossly underestimate your abusiveness? If so, why?

Adapted from: William Stacey and Anson Shupe, *The Family Secret: Domestic Violence in America*. Boston: Beacon Press, 1983, pp. 122-126.

connections between attitudes and actions. In relating the violent incident, the man not only develops some conscious assessment of his actions, but also identifies the feelings that accompany his outbursts. As the counselor inquires how the batterer felt at different points in the account ("How did you feel then?" as well as "How do you feel at this moment?"), he can prompt an awareness of the emotional and physical sensations that surround the violent behavior—cues that can serve as an "early warning" system to a potential attack.

Fourth, it is important that the counselor obtain some background information about the man. His education, marital history, religious background, military experience, mental and physical health, occupational status, and so on are helpful in assessing the batterer and determining if he needs assistance from a lawyer, psychologist, physician, or alcoholic counselor. It is also a means of getting more fully acquainted. Furthermore, careful records and documentation may be useful in resesarch or funding efforts.

Lastly, some programs prefer to pose contractual agreements with the men. Such contracts ensure that the expectations are clear and that a man does not drop out as soon as his wife returns. The new program participant is asked to sign a statement or make a verbal pledge to attend a required number of weekly sessions (generally 8-12). The short time commitment offers the man an attainable goal and the staff some basis on which to organize their curriculum. At the end of the required time, the man can enroll for another cycle of sessions or graduate to an advanced support group.

The prescribed time commitment should not suggest, however, that the man will be "cured" in a couple of months. The batterer, therefore, needs to know that he will most likely learn to restrain his behavior in the designated time frame, but that it will take months of hard work to achieve a substantial change in his behavior and the beginning of a new self-image. The wife, too, should be informed that the program does not work miracles. She should continue to protect herself and wait for a substantial change in her husband's behavior rather than accept his promises of program participation as evidence of a "change."

Staff members of the EMERGE program note that the group process evolves through a sequence of stages (Adams and McCormick, 1982). In the early stage (sessions 1-3), there is some homophobic anxiety expressed in talking tough and making wisecracks, and defensiveness manifested in projecting blame or degrading their wives. The men begin in the middle phase (sessions 4-18) to reveal more of their feelings and take more risks. They become introspective making connections between their socialization and their present behavior. It is in the latter phase (sessions 19-24) that the men's attitudes begin to change. They start to question their rigid sex role and seek more substantial bonds with each other and their wives. Some anxiety may also be expressed about the group's termination along with practical considerations for the future.

The contractual statement may, also, specify confidentiality and the behavior expected in the group. Some organizations ask the man and his spouse to sign a statement acknowledging the man's commitment to the program and the woman's awareness of the local shelter and its resources. Individually or together the two may set forth some short range goals that may include not yelling at the children when they are playing or smoking only a pack of cigarettes a week.

A determination of the fee and payment procedures should be made near the end of the interview. Most programs charge some fee based on a percentage of the man's salary. Deductions may also be factored in, such as the distance the man has to travel or the number of his dependents. Ideally, some portion of the payment should be collected before the man joins a group session. This practice offers a helpful reinforcement of the man's attendance. It should be made clear, however, that lack of money is not to be used as an excuse for not coming to a session.

Other straightforward ground rules are usually explained at this point: the men should call the program office, if they for some reason have to miss a meeting or arrive late. This courtesy helps the counselor keep track of the program's participants and affirms the participants' responsibility to the group. Also, the men are not to attend a meeting under the influence of drugs or alcohol, because it is important that they be thinking as clearly as possible during the meeting. Not smoking during the group meetings helps to keep men in touch with their emerging feelings, since many smoke to relax and avoid tension (see Table 4-7).

In closing, the interviewer might inquire about the man's current eating and sleeping habits. Many of the men who batter fall into a state of depression when their wives leave them that leads to personal neglect. It might be appropriate to inform the newcomer of other services in the area that he may contact for further assistance, such as the detoxification program, the mental health clinic, or the veterans' office.

Group Work

There are a number of ways to assign a newcomer to a counseling group. Most programs, however, have only one or two groups established and must arbitrarily assign a new participant to whatever group is available. Ideally, a man should be assigned to a group on the basis of his background, type of abuse and personal needs. For instance, a man whose wife has left, assigned to a group of men who are still living with their wives, may find it harder to get the needed support for his feelings of loss.

Some of the more established programs conveniently have four or five different groups meeting during the week and ask the new participant to visit at least two groups a week for three weeks. In this way, the man is maximally involved while he is the most desperate and is able to eventually select an on-going group that is comfortable to him.

Table 4-7: Ground Rules

These are some of the expectations for group sessions that should be explained to batterers during introductory interviews and reinforced during initial group meetings:

General

- Be on time—call if late or absent.

- No consumption of alcohol or drugs eight hours before meeting is allowed.

- Report any incidents of abuse or thoughts of suicide.

- Keep group discussion confidential.

- Only one person may smoke at a time.

- Make payments on time as agreed.

From: "Group Norms," MEN, Juneau, AK.

Group Discussions

- Speak for yourself: You need not represent the opinions of anyone else. Use "I" statements instead of generalizations.

- Be your own chairperson: When you are your own chairperson you are aware of your own needs and alert to the needs of others. You help see that only one person speaks at a time and talkers make time for listeners to speak. You are not free to do whatever you please.

- Avoid interviewing: If you need to ask someone about a personal issue, state your reason for the question. Interviewing can be a way of hiding your own struggles and can make others uncomfortable.

- Let disturbances take precedence: If you are feeling interference in "getting with" the group, say so. Let's see if we can work it out.

- Decide what you want from the group and act to get it: We are all in this together. There is plenty of time, help and care to go around.

From: Second Step, Pittsburgh, PA.

In any case, the program staff must decide on whether to maintain an open or closed group. Most programs have a closed admissions policy which sets a starting date for a group and does not allow new members in the group during the specified duration of sessions. A "closed" group can more easily develop a rapport among its members and a sequential curriculum of topics or exercises.

New clients, however, may have to wait several crucial weeks after their introductory interview in order for the new group to form. By the time the group starts they may have lost interest, feel their abuse has stopped, or committed more severe battering. The less established programs, moreover, often do not have enough men in the program to sustain a closed group. They have to assemble whomever is available in order to assure a meeting of at least a few men.

The "open" groups, on the other hand, allow members to enter an on-going group as soon after their first contact as possible and leave the group after attending the required number of sessions. The open groups provide a momentum that helps new members open-up and participate, but sometimes at the expense of group cohesiveness. The more experienced members can act as guides for the newer ones, explaining their progress as well as warning of the stumbling blocks. The veterans, in the process, gain a feeling of importance through initiating the new members into the program and helping them along.

Furthermore, a curriculum can be maintained even in the open groups. The weekly topics can be rotated so that any program participant will be exposed to the full cycle. The most crucial factor, anyway, is the men's discussion with other men about how to change their behavior and ultimately themselves.

As a compromise between open and closed groups, some programs like Men for Nonviolence in Fort Wayne have instituted a primary class for prospective group members. As soon as a batterer calls the program he is referred to the weekly hour-long instruction sessions. During these sessions the newcomer receives some information basic to domestic violence and important to the abuser. The "workshops," as Men for Nonviolence refers to them, comprise a series of four topic oriented meetings. The topics include a discussion of the terms "battery" and "violence," the expectations of masculinity and femininity in our society, the difficulty in expressing feelings, and the nature of assertive communication. In essence, the workshops condense some of the basic information outlined in the next chapter's discussion of group sessions objectives (see Frank and Houghton, 1982, for a basic education program designed for court-ordered counseling).

When a new closed group is formed, the men enter into a problem sharing and problem solving format that begins to explore more personally the information presented in the primary classes. They continue at the same time to attend the primary classes until they have attended the four topic presentations, regardless of when they start a closed group session. It does not matter when in the series of primary classes the men begin as long as they attend the full series.

Session Agenda

Most groups meet in a one-and-one-half to two hour session once during the week. Although the format and approach vary among programs, most generally begin with a twenty minute "check in" in which each member reports how he fared during the week and how he is feeling at the moment (see Table 4-8).

The counselors subsequently note the problems that warrant further discussion and may spend the next twenty minutes with a person who "needs time." A member of the group, for instance, may have abused his wife during the week or talked to her on the telephone only to feel enraged. The counselor will ask that person to talk about the incident in detail, much as was done during the introductory interview. As the abuser reviews the circumstances and his reactions, group members can offer their observations and suggestions and probe the speaker for more insight and possible

Table 4-8: Meeting Agenda

(Each item should require about 20 minutes)

• **Check-in:**	Each group member reports on the week's and present feelings.
• **Incident Recounting:**	A group member discusses a close call or incident of abuse.
• **Topic Discussion:**	A predetermined issue or an emerging theme is considered.
• **Didactic Exercise:**	Conduct an exercise that teaches skills or prompts awareness.
• **Closing:**	Affirm progress of the meeting, make weekly assignments, and establish buddy system.

• **Informal Socializing**

resolutions. The discussion of one incident will undoubtedly draw similar incidents or "close calls" from other members. Before long an instructive theme or issue may emerge.

In the next twenty minute period, the counselors can explore the theme more thoroughly or introduce a prearranged topic for discussion, like "responsibility for one's behavior" or "a man's role as provider."

Group exercises might be used to illustrate certain points or teach skills. A relaxation or guided imagery exercise, for example, might be used to teach the men how to defuse their stress. The counselor may demonstrate the use of "self-talk" or "time outs" as a means of alleviating anger. There are a variety of exercises, too, with language and posturing that can illustrate the male propensity for domination and control (see Chapter 5).

Some activity is often used to mark the end of the meeting, as well. The counselor may ask for each member's objectives for the coming week and affirm that abuse is wrong and it must stop. One program uses a quiet meditation period in which each member looks at the others as a reminder of the group's accomplishments and support. Buddy assignments might be given for the coming week; the men select a partner to telephone to offer encouragement or a helpful reminder. Lastly, after or before the meeting it is helpful to have some time for informally socializing and developing friendships. In the process, the men begin to form a reference group beyond their work or sport acquaintances who often ridicule their efforts to change (see Table 4-9).

Problem Areas

Within an open or closed group, some distinct problem areas emerge that warrant special attention: withholding, denial, blaming, depression, and dropout. From my observation, these often appear in sequence for groups or for individuals (see Table 4-10 for summary). In a sense, each is a more sophisticated form of defense, so as one resistance is outdone, an abuser may escalate to the next one. Each defense is a means of avoiding responsibility for one's behavior and the need to change, but the defenses are often employed so unconsciously and earnestly that both the counselor and the group participants unwittingly tolerate them. The counselor needs to be particularly alert, therefore, to recognize these problem areas and respond to them decisively, if he is to keep the group and its individuals progressing.

Table 4-9: Guidelines Toward Achieving Buddyship

1. Begin by articulating those attributes which you respect in another man and those which you dislike.

    The positive attributes should include personality characteristics that generate joy, the freedom to be yourself, a willingness to open up and reveal yourself as a person, a sense of trust and safety, a desire to be talkative, humorous, and silly, an eagerness to explore, expand, and risk, and a receptiveness to learning new things when you are around that person.

    The negative attributes would include characteristics that tend to make you feel pessimistic, distrustful, guarded, inhibited, uncreative, bored, depressed, resentful, and scared about life when you are in that person's presence.

2. Draw a social nexus chart which pictures yourself in the center and the men that you consider potential buddies in circles around you. Place those you feel closest to nearest yourself and those you feel more distant from in circles which are progressively further away.

3. Now define in *specific* terms the characteristics you like and dislike about each. The following questions may be helpful to you in doing this:

    a)   Is he guarded and secretive around me and do I feel guarded and secretive around him? In other words, do I feel like I'm prying whenever I ask him something personal? Do I feel anxious and regretful when I tell him something intimate about myself? Does he volunteer personal information about himself freely when he's around me and do I feel a strong desire to be open about myself when I'm around him?

    b)   Do I feel comfortable calling him and would he call me up for no other reason than to say hello?

    c)   Do I feel comfortable going over to see him on the spur of the moment, or do I feel I have to plan each meeting with him carefully and well in advance and only for a specific reason such as golfing?

    d)   Do I feel respected and appreciated when I'm around him and do I respect and admire him?

    e)   Do I have envious and competitive feelings toward him and do I sense that he has similar feelings toward me?

f)   Does he say and do things that embarrass me and do I seem to make him uncomfortable?

g)   Would I feel comfortable asking him to drive me to the airport, lend me his car, or give me a place to sleep when I needed that? Would I feel comfortable doing these things for him?

h)   Would I feel safe and confident if he were alone with my girl friend or wife and would I feel comfortable knowing that I could resist the temptation to seduce his girl friend or wife without his knowledge when he wasn't around?

i)   Do I feel I can grow, learn, and become more through a relationship with him and do I feel that I can provide the same kind of atmosphere and opportunity for him?

j)   Am I eager to know him as a total person or am I just interested in him to share a specific activity and would otherwise prefer not to get close to him?

4. Once you have determined who is a potential buddy, recognize that two of the areas of greatest difficulty are those of trust and of dominance.

To handle the area of trust ask your potential buddy to define vulnerable areas with you; the kinds of behaviors that would destroy confidence and good feeling in both of you. Begin with the milder ones such as, for example, a show of indifference in him when you are discussion something of great importance to you. (One man mentioned to me his anger and diminished trust at a friend whose one ear was glued to the radio listening to a football wrap-up show while he was trying to discuss serious problems.) Then go progressively to the more sensitive areas such as making derogatory comments about you in front of close friends, not backing you up in an argument with others, revealing something personal to others which you had told him in confidence, or being seductive with a woman you care about.

To handle the issue of dominance, work toward equalizing power and decision-making so that neither of you winds up in the shadow of the other. Arrange tag-along meetings where one afternoon or evening you share in an experience of interest to him and then have him tag-along doing something which involves an area of your strength and interest.

5. Share your respective experiences of past disappointments and hurts in other friendships. Discuss incidents that have previously impaired or destroyed friendships for both of you as a way of learning about each other's areas of vulnerability and sensitivity.

6. Get together on a regular basis, perhaps once a month, a time specifically set aside to keep your relationship up to date and to avoid hidden injustice collecting. At this time discuss any incident or remarks that were made by either of you which caused disappointment or discomfort. In other words, be open with each other regarding areas of abrasion *before* they create great rifts.

From: Herb Goldberg, *The Hazards of Being Male.* New York: Signet Books, 1976, pp. 138-140.

Table 4-10: Problems Encountered in Group Counseling

Problem	Symptoms	Intervention
1. Withholding	Guarded thoughts and feelings Deflection of questions Generalizing and vagaries Resistance to self-disclosure Unload in monologue	Counselor disclosure Members' introduction Two-person exercises Request observations and comments
2. Denial	Deny guilt and responsibility for abuse Minimize violence by claiming not severe Rationalize by explaining the complications Externalize by blaming some other factor like alcohol	Note discrepancies and add contrary facts Assert axiom of one's responsibility for own behavior Affirm that men can change
3. Blaming	Use wives as scapegoats Accuse women of provocation Criticism of women's movement Increased self-pity	Reminder that responsible for own behavior Note facts on women's status Challenge men to organize and make constructive changes Identify underlying feelings of self-pity De-escalate debate
4. Depression	Feelings of loneliness Miss wife and children Personal neglect and insomnia Lack of motivation and interest Thoughts of suicide	Crisis counseling on phone Vigorous assertions of a positive nature List of "cans" to reflect on Instruction in positive self-talk Phone call from other group members Assign helpful work task
5. Dropout	Late or absent at meetings Announce not need program Assert can solve own problems	Follow-up calls Reminder of commitment to program Mention of previous payment Offer individual counseling Sternly reprimand for "copping out" Work for societal support of nonviolence in men

Withholding

Early in the sessions, men are particularly likely to withhold their thoughts and feelings. This is due, in part, to the initial tension that accompanies any interaction among strangers. However, in many cases, the guarded posturing is related to the nature of masculinity itself. Counselors of men in general note that men go into "hiding" when expected to share their feelings (Scher, 1982). Disclosing one's feelings may make a man appear vulnerable, weak, or feminine. Men may attempt to maintain control by not sharing.

A counselor's effort to model expressive behavior—be emotional, intuitive, creative, open, sensitive, touching and hugging—can go a long way in encouraging expressiveness in others. As the counselors work particularly to disclose their own feelings and establish close relationships, the men will feel less threatened and more inclined to participate. Giving each man the opportunity to tell something about themselves, however superficial, can also develop familiarity and open the doors for further discussion. Furthermore, role playing or two-person exercises can help the men to move out of themselves.

In sum, the counselor must be prepared under these circumstances to take the initiative to draw out the members. It is important, however, that the counselor be sensitive to the withholding and not be offended by it. If, in desperation, he attempts to order or instruct the men into participation, he risks infringing on the men's need for control and making them withdraw further.

As the members begin to open up, it is not uncommon for them to go to the other extreme and "unload" their problems. Like popping a cork off a champagne bottle, a man will burst forth with an unstoppable stream of feelings which has long been buried or neglected. His monologue is often another form of control. It allows the speaker to say only what he wants and avoid answering questions. In this sense, the unloading is not only used as a

self-indulgent "release," but also as a further defense against
challenge and change. As important as it is to support this expression, the counselor must, therefore, interrupt periodically to prevent the speaker from monopolizing the meeting and others from
losing interest.

The group members in these initial meetings will, moreover,
tend to speak directly to the counselors rather than risk involvement with the group. Even their questions about another group
member may be posed to a counselor instead of directly to the
person in question. The counselor, in this case, needs to direct
the speakers to address the entire group or a particular member
of the group rather than the counselor. By asking questions like
"What do you think of that, John?", he can teach the men better
communication and build the interaction that will eventually carry
the group.

Denial

Those who work with abusers unanimously agree that these
men tend to deny their guilt and responsibility. They may feel sorry
that they lost control and got themselves in the mess they did, but
they are often not prepared to accept the pain their abuse has
brought to others.

Consequently, the abusers may *minimize* the impact of their
violence: "Oh, it really didn't hurt that much. I just gave her a
little shove and now she has gone and made a big deal of it." Or,
they may deny it through *rationalization*: "Well, she had it coming.
If she hadn't been nagging me so, I wouldn't have hit her."
Externalizing is another means of denying. In this mode the batterer
blames some external factor for his violence, like alcohol or his
job: "I couldn't help it. It is all the way I was brought up," or
"I really didn't know what I was doing, because I was so drunk."

A counselor can often break through such denial by tactfully
noting the discrepancies or adding contrary facts to the man's story.
In this way, he may present the sort of cognitive dissonance in

which the batterer has to adjust his version to maintain some consistency. The counselor may simply explain that the individual is the only one who is responsible for his feelings, thoughts and behavior. Most men do want their circumstances to change, so appealing to this axiom of responsibility can be appreciated. It not only says "You can do it!", but also that one can develop an authentic sense of control.

Blaming

Blaming women is a related form of avoidance. Upon first joining a group, a man will often be noticeably contrite, perhaps even flaying himself with self-criticism. This can be explained as part of the cycle of violence: for a short period after a violent incident, the abuser is generally ashamed and apologetic; as time elapses, he believes the violence will not occur again and excuses himself; but his tensions gradually accumulate until he explodes again. However, as the men become more comfortable with the group and more accepting of their own behavior, they inevitably blame women for their problems.

The abusers begin to recognize that they have been "set up," so to speak. The way they were coddled by their mothers, disciplined by their female school teachers, or manipulated by their wives seems to contribute to how they presently behave toward women. Furthermore, the men see particularly the women's movement as now agitating women to oppose men. The abuser's awareness turns, therefore, to resentment and then becomes self-pity. They claim that women today are getting all the breaks, while men are made to bear the brunt of the changes. After all, women have their own shelters, the backing of the courts and police, sympathy of social workers, and never consider what the man may be going through—or so the men argue.

The counselor obviously needs to challenge this scapegoating. To begin, they can remind the men that they are responsible for their own behavior. They also may appraise the men of the facts which show that women have not made gains over men. Moreover, the men's complaints about women's liberation can serve as a stepping stone for their own social action. The counselor can explain that the women have shelters for battered women and "orders of protection," in particular, because they worked together for them. It can be pointed out that men can bring about some constructive changes, too, if they would organize instead of competing or feeling sorry for themselves.

During the blaming, the traditional male camaraderie may prevail in the group, leading the group members to oppose the counselor for sticking up for women. The outnumbered counselor can switch the attention away from the women and back to the feelings of the individual members, being careful to address individuals rather than appear to be impersonally lecturing the whole group. He might accomplish this by simply reflecting the mood of the group: "So what I am hearing is that you are feeling sorry for yourself." The counselor in this line of fire may find that rather than fight back with some sort of heady rebuttal, it is better to de-escalate the discussion and return to the matter later. In this way, he demonstrates one more alternative to prideful bickering—bickering that for many men can lead to violence.

Depression

As mentioned, many of the men fall into severe depression shortly after a battering incident, especially when their wife leaves them. They become lonely and miss terribly their wife and family for three reasons. One is that their wives, and before them their mothers, took care of them. Many of the men simply do not know how to do their dirty laundry or cook a substantial meal. A second reason is that a man's identity is attached to being the provider and boss of a family. The home may, in fact, be his only arena of authority and status. To lose this, is to lose his manhood and his sense of worth.

For a third reason, a wife's departure often confronts many of the men with their problem for the first time. The men are left to examine themselves and this is often a painful and unsettling process. A "What's the use?" attitude consequently appears. Some abusers mention not caring about anything or not feeling motivated to change. Some men may even talk of suicide. To end it all in a car accident seems better, the men claim, than going through the humiliation of being exposed as a "wife beater" and outdone by a woman who dared to leave. A few of the men may, moreover, become frantically desperate and attempt to retrieve their wives through threats and manipulation.

A counselor may, therefore, find it necessary to spend a good deal of time offering crisis counseling over the phone. The batterer may require some vigorous assertions to break his downward spiral. The counselor can insist that the man can change and make life better for himself and others or that he should take a long, lively walk. He cannot promise, of course, what the man most wants to hear—that he will get his wife back.

Some programs offer a list of "I can's" to each participant to reflect on in moments of discouragement. Others offer some instruction in positive "self talk" in which the man essentially gives himself a lecture about his good qualities and capabilities. It may also be helpful to have other members of a group call the depressed person and remind him of the possibilities for change. Often getting the man to do something for someone else can redirect the preoccupation with his problems. Many of the men have a talent at repairing cars, fixing furniture, or doing carpentry that can be of help to someone in the program or the community. If the depression appears to be a chronic problem, the batterer should, of course, be referred to a doctor or therapist.

Dropout

Perhaps the greatest challenge that faces a men's program, as it does many social services, is the dropout. Even the best men's programs have 25% of the men leaving the program within the first few weeks. It is not uncommon for the dropout rate to be as high as fifty percent by the end of the required time commitment. Furthermore, less than half of those who remain will choose to continue in a follow-up program.

There are, of course, a number of factors that contribute to this phenomenon. One, the loose screening allows men to enter a program who are not fully committed to it. Two, many of the men get what they want within only a few sessions. Their wives may return to them out of feelings of regret or because they are encouraged by the husband's contacting the program. Three, some of the men are terribly threatened by the prospects of having to open up in front of strangers. Their insecurity is intensified by admitting their problems and realizing that they must do something about them. Four, men will occasionally announce that they are not going to return as a means of testing the group's support and respect, or as a power play to show that they are still in charge.

A counselor can attempt to check the absences and dropouts from the program in several ways. Most programs place at least one follow-up call to an absentee. (Calling more than once or twice, however, may be perceived as hassling the abuser and push him away for good.) Sometimes, there is a legitimate problem that the counselor can address; other times the show of concern is enough to reignite the dropout's interest. If not, the counselor has a right to remind the man of his commitment to the group and his obligation to call if he is not going to attend. The partial payment for the entire set of sessions made during the introductory interview may also supply a persuasive argument: "You might as well come and get your money's worth since there are no refunds."

Supportive one-to-one counseling may be what is needed to help some men through the initial uneasiness. The abuser may simply be more comfortable talking to an individual than to the group. Of course, some of the dropouts need to be more sternly confronted. At this stage the man is going to dropout anyway, so taking a chance with a forceful reprimand is of little risk. The counselor may also want to remind the abuser of the cycle of violence and the likelihood of being violent again. The counselor may directly accuse the man of dropping out because he is frightened and insecure. Ironically, the confrontation may present an irresistible challenge to the abuser. Or, it may regain the dropout's respect by demonstrating that the counselor can be manly, too, and stand up to the batterer on his own terms.

There is, however, no foolproof strategy for retaining men in a counseling program. The threat of having to change a lifetime of behavior is difficult in itself. The sanctions that tolerate violence, as well as stigmatize men for being non-violent, are a more severe obstacle and beyond the realm of most programs. Program attendance is not likely, therefore, to stabilize until it becomes more socially acceptable for men in general to address their tendency toward violence and abuse. Ideally, as more men go through programs gaining confidence and a new self image, they will feel compelled to organize against the social norms reinforcing violent behavior. Then, more men will not only come forward for help, but will also stay with the programs they join.

5

Counseling Processes

The supervised self-help approach advocated in this book incorporates aspects identified with the social service as well as the social action orientations, discussed in Chapter 1. This chapter offers a brief rationale for this supervised form of self-help counseling and then outlines an eight phase approach. The approach integrates the prevailing strategies of several existing programs for men who batter into these eight specific objectives: taking responsibility, breaking isolation, avoiding violent behavior, reducing stress, communicating feelings, resolving conflict, undoing sex role stereotypes, and organizing social action (see Table 5-1). The emphasis of the social service oriented programs tends to be on the first few objectives, while the social action oriented programs tend to emphasize the last few.

The eight objectives comprise a sequential curriculum that leads the batterer from acceptance of his problem, to stopping his abuse, and then on to addressing social supports of his violence. In closed groups, one of the weekly sessions might be devoted to one of the objectives. In open groups portions of several objectives might be incorporated into one week's session and other aspects introduced the next week. With portions of four different objectives presented each week, group members would eventually be exposed entirely to all eight objectives regardless of when they join or depart from a group.

Table 5-1: Teaching Self-Help

Objective	Techniques	Precautions
1. Accepting Responsibility	Violence Witness Survey (Table 5-2)	Use of social awareness to justify behavior or self-pity
	Battered Women Quiz (Table 5-3)	
	"What Is Violence?" Questionnaire (Table 5-4)	
2. Breaking Isolation	Open-Ended Questionnaire (Table 5-5)	
	Self-Help Group Participation	Men's groups tendency toward instrumental ends and simply solutions
3. Avoiding Violent Behavior	Time-Outs (Table 5-6)	
	Anger Log (Table 5-7)	Assumption that anger control is a "cure"
4. Reducing Stress	Guided Imagery Exercise (Table 5-8)	
	Relaxation Exercises Positive Self-Talk	Stress as avoidance of deep-seated existential dilemmas
	Dealing With Potential Stress (Table 5-9)	
5. Communicating Feelings	"I feel . . ." Statements	Use of assertiveness to manipulate wife more effectively
	Feeling Log	
	Assertiveness Training (Table 5-10)	
	Saying "No" Role Plays	
6. Resolving Conflict	Rules For Fighting Fair (Table 5-11)	Maneuvering to get own way rather than concede power
	Problem Solving Exercise (Table 5-12)	
	"Plan of Action" Role Plays	
	Group Consultation	

7. Undoing Sex Role Stereotypes	Women Speakers	Intellectualizing of sexism issues
	Films of Abuse (Appendix)	
	Language Exercise (Table 5-13)	
	Macro-Analysis Diagram (Table 5-14)	
	Chart of Household Duties	
8. Taking Social Action	Conversion Process	Become overzealous or self-serving
	Assignment of Helping Task	
	Attend Social Action Coalition	
	Participation in Program Functions	
	Public Speaking on Abuse	
	Organize Social Action Group	

The Supervised Self-Help Group

Most existing programs for men who batter have developed a counseling approach designed to address specifically the causes of wife abuse. Many of the techniques, exercises, and skills have been adopted from conventional psychotherapy but are tailored to suit the special needs of batterers. The basic thrust of the approach is to teach the abusers to regulate their own behavior. The aim is, fundamentally, to help the men learn how to help themselves.

As previously discussed, the men perceive participation in conventional counseling as a sign of weakness; consequently, the self-help group is a preferred way to help resistant men to discuss their problems. Conventional "self-help" groups bring together individuals with a common problem to give each other support, encouragement and constructive criticism. In the process, the group members break down the sense of isolation and gain a feeling of confidence and self-control. Significantly, the individuals learn to take responsibility for changing their own behavior, since they do not have a therapist or expert to rely upon—all they have are others like themselves. (Often a group facilitator is designated to guide the group discussion, but usually this person is without professional training and does not provide therapy.)

Most abuser programs add a trained counselor to this self-help process. Some professional expertise is warranted because of the life-threatening circumstances that accompany abuse. The counselor must vigilantly monitor the risk to women and children. In the process, he is likely to encounter complex legal and mental health issues that a group facilitator would not necessarily be equipped to handle. Therefore, the self-help groups for men who batter should be more carefully supervised than groups such as Alcoholics Anonymous. Wife abuse is a crime, whereas alcoholic consumption is not. The violence of a batterer also directly injures family members, whereas alcohol abuse affects others indirectly.

A trained counselor is also needed to direct the interaction and offer instruction to the self-help group. As discussed in

Chapter 4, batterers tend to carry entrenched defenses to the group that often require uprooting by an experienced staff person. If these defenses are not effectively confronted, the group may unwittingly reinforce abusive behavior or undermine some members' efforts to change.

Moreover, groups are not as likely to progress through the eight counseling objectives without the support of a trained counselor. Each successive objective builds on the previous one and demands more initiative and more substantial change from the batterer. Without a counselor to encourage and prod the group members, they may not accept the extent of the changes required as well as resist the task if they are aware of it. Once aware, they may tend to resist the task of changing if not urged along by the counselor. As mentioned, groups of men who batter often digress into women blaming or self-pity. The instrumental concerns of most men, furthermore, would cause many to drop out as soon as they gain some control of their anger.

1. Accepting Responsibility

As mentioned in the previous chapter, abusers are reluctant to admit that they have a problem and to accept responsibility for the behavior. Therefore, the first step in counseling men who batter is to help them take responsibility for their behavior. When they admit that they have a problem, they are more likely to accept help. As long as the men perceive the source of the action to be something external—a wife's nagging or the result of drinking,—they are unlikely to accept that there is anything wrong with them or that changing themselves will do any good.

Men in general, of course, find self-disclosure of personal shortcomings difficult. This is true, in part, because of the socialization that would have them keep "in charge." To admit to their own shortcomings is to admit weakness and a loss of their competitive edge. Moreover, many men who batter believe that they have done nothing wrong; they are supposed to keep their wives in line.

In many cases, the abusers' egos are too weak to accept their faults. The men consequently blame their wives to protect themselves from being labeled "a wife beater." Wife beaters, they believe, are men who have failed in marriage and in manhood. Even though a man may be entitled to hit a woman, resorting to abuse is stooping pretty low. A man should never let his wife get so out of his control in the first place, or so the logic goes. Moreover, they know that after the abusive incident, the victim can make trouble for her abuser. Many men, therefore, feel that they have to abuse further to prevent retaliation. Thus, one act of abuse inevitably leads to others.

As mentioned, one way to begin to offset the abuser's avoidance is with the Violent Behavior Inventory (see Table 4-5). The results of the questionnaire can be used to demonstrate the extent and nature of an individual's violence. In subsequent sessions, the abuser should be alerted to the context of his violence. As a man begins to see that he is part of a violent culture, he realizes that it is not "just him." He consequently feels less embarrassed to admit his faults and more inclined to better himself.

Several exercises are useful for this purpose. One possibility is the Violence Witness Survey (see Table 5-2). This survey asks a man to recall the kind and amount of abuse witnessed while growing up. Questions about abuse between parents, toward him from his parents, among siblings and among friends are included in the survey. The results can illustrate that the violent behavior of others may be serving as a model for the abuser's present behavior. In sum, the exercise suggests that much of the violence is learned. If it is learned, it is something that can be unlearned, that is, changed. The fear of admitting one's violence is eased, since the violence appears not as a fixed part of the man's identity, but more as an outgrowth of socialization.

Table 5-2: Violence Witness Survey: Childhood Experiences of Violence

Instructions:

What is your age? _____ . What is your gender? M F

Make a check mark if you have seen or experienced the following between:

	Your parents	Parent and you or your brother or sister	You and your sister or brother	Your brothers or sisters	You and others	Others (not TV)
Verbal Abuse						
Throw Something						
Push or Shove						
Slap or Spank						
Kick or Punch						
Beat Up						
Use or Threaten to use a Weapon						
Unwanted Sexual Contact or Abuse						

From: Sojourner Truth House, Milwaukee, WI.

The Battered Women Quiz is another resource which might be used to measure the nature and extent of wife abuse (see Table 5-3). This series of true-false questions can confront men with misconceptions about domestic violence and lead to a frank discussion of abuse as a social problem. Again, this exercise can alert the abuser to the fact that he is not alone.

Exploring the question, "What is violence," can also be helpful in building awareness (see Table 5-4). In a series of open-ended questions, the men are asked to define various kinds of violence. Their definitions of violence, of course, will vary with some men developing definitions that exclude their particular behavior or minimizing it with euphemisms. (A slap, for instance, may be described as "a corrective gesture.") Contrasting the group members written responses can expose these tendencies. In the process, the counselor might draw attention to the disclaimers and euphemisms used during the Viet Nam War to make the military look less sinister to the critical public, and inquire how the batterers' definitions differ from our government's. (For example, fire bombing the countryside and incinerating innocent villagers and their fields was termed "strategic defoliation.")

Throughout the program, however, the men must be reminded that they are *responsible* for their behavior and also that they *can* do something about it. Excuses and projections will no doubt slip into conversation and need to be challenged. The counselor needs to be alert especially that men do not use this social awareness to justify their behavior or indulge in self pity. ("Everybody else is doing it, so I'm just going along with the crowd!") These reactions are simply modifications of the avoidance. As suggested in the previous chapter, some individuals may have to be more forcefully confronted if they continue to distort or deflect the purpose of the exercises. Nevertheless, most of the men eventually appreciate being challenged on the debilitating avoidance. They do not want to lose control of their lives or be manipulated by repressive social forces; most do want to be themselves and encounter others as they really are. However, at this point, they do not know how.

Table 5-3: Battered Women Quiz

Directions: Please answer these questions with a True or False response.

1. Twenty percent of all Americans approve of hitting a spouse on appropriate occasions (Harris Poll). _____

2. Household violence is most likely to occur in the evenings and on the weekends. _____

3. The percentage of persons approving hitting decreased among college educated Americans (Harris Poll). _____

4. Many police officers are injured on family disturbance calls—approximately 30% of police injuries are from such calls. _____

5. Battering is more common in lower income families. _____

6. Alcohol is a fundamental cause of battering. _____

7. Single women have worse mental and emotional health than married women (Cited in Tavris and Offir, 1977). _____

8. Men are more likely to help a woman being attacked by a man than a man being attacked by another man. _____

9. An old town ordinance specifies that no husband shall beat his wife after 10 p.m. at night or on Sunday (Pennsylvania). _____

10. A husband is more likely to kill his wife than vice versa. _____

11. About 50% of all battering instances are reported.
    _____

12. Battering occurs more often when couples are not married.
    _____

13. Most women who leave a situation where they have been severely battered do not return to live in the home. _____

14. Most physical abuse is preceded by verbal arguments (Dobash and Dobash, 1979). _____

15. Most battering is done with fists rather than with an open hand. _____

16. More wives are currently being sought as runaways than are husbands (Tracers Company of America)._____

17. Battering usually does not begin until later in marriage—after the fifth or sixth year of marriage. _____

18. As many as ⅓ of the men who batter women have been involved with the military. _____

19. Physical abuse is a factor in 40% of the divorces in working class families (Woman's Day). _____

20. Approximately 2 million women will be battered this year.
    _____

21. Early life experiences are the single greatest factor contributing to wife battering. _____

22. In some states a woman may make a civil suit against her husband to sue him for loss of wages if she is unable to work because of battering (Colorado). _____

23. A woman should wash off any blood, clean herself up, and regain composure before going to the police to file charges after a beating. _____

24. About ⅓ of all assaultive crime complaints are filed by victims of domestic violence (Washtenaw County, MI).

_____

25. Over 60% of domestic violence victims have been victims in previous assaults. _____

Answers: Questions 2, 4, 9, 15, 16, 18, 19, 20, 21, 22, 24, 25 are TRUE.

From: Linda White, Virginia Neal Blue Women's Resource Center, Grand Junction, CO 81501; and Deborah Cowing, ed., Domestic Violence Project, Ann Arbor, MI 48104.

Table 5-4: "What is Violence?" Questionnaire

Directions: Please answer the following questions and bring them to the next group meeting.

NAME _____

1. What is violence?

2. What is domestic violence?

3. What are some kinds of domestic violence?

4. What is stress?

5. What are some stressful experiences for you?

6. How do you know when you are feeling stress?

7. What are some ways to cope with stress?

8. What percentage of families experience some form of domestic violence?

From: MEN, Juneau, AK.

2. Breaking Isolation

Helping men who batter realize what they have in common with other men and develop relationships with other men is a vital step in introducing them to the possibilities of change. The social isolation most men experience contributes to men's denial and to their anger. The competition which men learn to accept and thrive on precludes close relationships, as indicated in the discussion about male socialization found in Chapter 2. In an effort to appear in control and competitive, men tend to resist disclosing their weaknesses or their emotions. Consequently, many men are resistant to mutual support and criticism that might facilitate personal change.

Preliminary studies of wife abuse show the battered woman and the man who batters to be "isolated." The female victims are frequently physically and emotionally isolated. They have few substantial social contacts outside the family to offer them moral or financial support. In other words, the women are trapped in the abusive relationship with no place to turn. The male batterers, on the other hand, are more emotionally than physically isolated. As breadwinners, they control the family finances in a manner that allows them relative independence. Also, their children are more attached to their mother, allowing the men more mobility. However, the men seldom achieve relationships that offer substantial emotional support. They may organize in service clubs, sport teams, or professional associations, but these organizations are more concerned with accomplishing tasks than building relationships.

Men in general have fewer bonds with friends, relatives, and neighbors than women. According to studies of social networks (Warren, 1981), these "informal" relationships lead individuals to "formal" social services. Men, therefore, are less likely to find their way to professional help. They most often are left to fend for themselves. This isolation obviously needs to be broken down, if men are to seek help and begin to change.

There are several ways to help an abuser move from emotional isolation to mutual support. Questionnaires, like the Battered Women Quiz and Violence Witness Survey mentioned in the previous section, illustrate what men have in common with others. Chapter 4 also presents a number of techniques that help men break their isolation: check-in's, incident review, and post-session socializing.

Open-ended questionnaires can also be helpful in breaking down walls of isolation (see Table 5-5). Questions like "One thing I like about myself . . ." guide men toward feelings that they can safely convey to others. Filling out a written questionnaire gives the men time to think through their answers and prepare to present them orally. It allows them to mentally rehearse their response. The answers from individual group members should contain some similarities and can be used to start a discussion. The group session in this way becomes not only a source of self-knowledge, but also a kind of social oracle exposing common concerns.

Nevertheless, the most decisive way to break the isolation is to involve the abuser directly with other men who have similar problems. For this reason a self-help group is an essential component in counseling men who batter. In the process of meeting and talking with other men, the abusers develop relationships that lead them to share not only information but also personal feelings. As they learn to share more of their emotions with other men, it should become easier to share them with family members and eventually fellow workers. Men who are involved in such self-help groups are less likely to repress tensions and anger which often erupt in violence at home.

Many of the self-help programs, in fact, develop an identity of their own that makes belonging to RAVEN, for instance, similar to belonging to the Elks, Eagles, or Lions Clubs. The self-help group appeals to the "masculine tendency" to organize in service groups (Tiger, 1969) but intends to promote personal and social change rather than extend male influence and prominence. The

Table 5-5: Open-Ended Questionnaire

When we were first married _____

_____

_____

One thing I want from my wife is _____

_____

_____

When I abuse my wife _____

_____

_____

The opposite of abuse is _____

_____

_____

When I'm angry at my wife and don't abuse her I _____

_____

_____

_____

One thing I like about myself is _____

_____

_____

If I didn't have to please my wife I _____

_____

_____

When I feel abused I _____

_____

_____

If I had my way I'd _____

_____

_____

From: Second Step, Pittsburgh, PA.

batterer program ideally help men not to obtain more power and control, but to give up some of it.

There is, however, an obvious precaution that needs to be heeded. Because of the tendency to organize in groups for instrumental ends, it is important that the counselors keep the self-help group from trying to manage an overly simple solution. The objective of the group is to move men toward a cooperative process of self-disclosure and mutual support, rather than toward manipulative competition for personal gain and status.

3. Avoiding Violent Behavior

Men who batter need to be taught early in the program just how to avoid being violent—especially if they are still living with their wives. As suggested in Chapter 2, one way to control this behavior is to become more aware of one's anger and learn to express the full range of one's emotions. In this way, a man can redirect, diffuse, and avoid anger. But in the meantime, steps can be taken to avoid the violent behavior associated with anger. The abuser may, in the process, discover that he does not have to be violent when he is angry. Men should in fact understand that it is all right to be angry—just as it is all right to be joyful or sad— but that it is not all right to be violent.

The relationship of anger to violence is, of course, a complex matter which emotive, cognitive, and behavioral psychologists interpret differently. Nevertheless, the emotion of anger is generally thought to be the impetus for the violent behavior. Therefore, many psychologists and counselors encourage men who batter to "control their anger" in order to stop the violent behavior. This objective, however, can be easily translated into further containment and repression of one's emotions, because so many men are pre-occupied with the issue of control (see the conclusion of Chapter 3).

Interestingly, recent studies on anger (Tavris, 1983) do indicate that controlling one's anger may be beneficial, despite the popular notion to "let it all hang out." According to much of the research on the subject, letting anger run its course merely reinforces and often escalates the feeling of anger rather than dissipate it. It also incurs the risk of provoking retaliation or inflicting injury or resentment. Therefore, even counting to ten may allow time for some angry people to diffuse the anger and avoid a violent or aggressive outburst.

The point, however, is not that anger should be merely contained or repressed. As previously discussed, anger does appear to underlie the violent behavior of most batterers, but the violence is related to a matrix of social factors (see Table 3-2). An accumulation of negative emotions leads to a feeling of displeasure, pain, and eventually indignation that is likely to be expressed in a range of violent actions. The instigation of the angry feelings could be a combination of events that occurred at work, with relatives, or in the home. This anger is often turned into aggressive acts directed towards one's wife because of sex role socialization and the patriarchal sanctions which endorse violence against women.

Most programs initially provide men with a few techniques that help them to avoid this violence. These techniques are helpful, however, only if the men are sufficiently motivated to use the techniques and aware enough of their anger to respond to it. To attain both acceptance of the notion that women should not be beaten as well as awareness of one's angry feelings often requires time and work in itself. Consequently, the men must be precautioned that techniques can be a dangerous crutch, if the men are not simultaneously working to make substantial changes in their perceptions. Otherwise, in our technique oriented world, the men may learn a few practical ways to offset their violence and leave the program believing that they have what they need to stop battering.

As discussed in the previous chapter, "incident reviews" can help men identify "cues" that accompany their anger or violence (see Table 5-6). Their body tells them that they are angry with a tight neck, sweaty palms, firm lips, taut face, or the like. The cues may be behavioral, as well as physical, like turning away and mumbling. As soon as these cues appear, the man must heed the signal by calling for a "time-out"—a technique that most all programs recommend in one form or another. The man might simply say to his partner, "I feel angry and need a 'time-out,'" or he might indicate by making a "T" sign with his hands that he is about to leave. The "T" sign is often recommended because it precludes the man's talking and risking escalating his anger or becoming involved in an argument.

The man must immediately leave for one hour—no if's, and's or but's. (There is a temptation to return to the house as soon as the initial intensity subsides or stay out too long as a means of getting back at the woman.) In the interim, the man should avoid driving or drinking, but rather take a brisk walk in order to ease tension and stimulate thought. He may stop on the way to call a friend, a crisis phone line, or his "buddy" in the group. Talking about his anger is another means to defuse it short of violence. The conversation, as well, can give the man needed perspectives on his situation.

Upon returning to the house, the man should promptly "check-in" with his wife asserting how he is feeling and explaining the reasons for it. The intent should not be to change the other person's behavior but to "unload one's basket" of gripes. Each partner presenting their gripes, even if they are not resolved, helps remove some of the unexpressed feelings that would otherwise accumulate and clarifies the source of one's feelings. Ultimately, the man needs to change his images of himself and of women. Modifying these images may help him to maintain more realistic expectations and find greater satisfaction.

Many programs require men to maintain a written Anger Log, as well. In the Anger Log, the men are to identify the situation, cues, their response, and feelings (see Table 5-7). For some men, this procedure is a bit schoolish, making them feel like a student or child—something that insults their fragile egos. A journal, nevertheless, provides continuity from meeting to meeting and an

Table 5-6: Avoiding Violence With a "Time-Out"

The following are a sequence of steps that can help avoid a violent outburst:

1. Recognize physical or behavioral "cues" that signal you are intensely angry.

2. Assert immediately "I need to take a time-out" or make a "T" sign with your hands without speaking.

3. Leave the house for a full hour to cool off and collect your thoughts.

4. Take a brisk walk and call a crisis phone line, good friend, or "buddy" from the program. (Do not drink, drive, or go to a bar!)

5. Return to the house in one hour—no sooner or later.

6. Check-in with your wife and talk about how you feel and why. (Don't try to change her behavior; simply start by airing your gripes.)

7. Report and discuss the close call at the next group meeting.

Adapted from: Daniel Sonkin and Michael Durphy, *Learning To Live Without Violence*. San Francisco: Volcano Press, 1982, p. 14.

Table 5-7: Anger Log

Date

1. **Anger Event**
    What was the situation?
    What did you get angry about?

2. **Anger Level**
    On a scale from 1-10 were
    you mad, angry or raging?

3. **Physical and Behavior Cues**
    What sensations or actions
    preceded your anger?

4. **"I feel . . ." Statements**
    What were your underlying
    feelings (hurt, sadness,
    fear, etc.)

5. **Self Talk**
    What can you say to yourself
    to bring this particular
    anger level down?

6. **Behavioral Response**
    How did the situation actually
    end? Did you take a time out,
    do some physical activity, or
    use drugs or alcohol before or
    after the incident?

7. **Prevention**
    If a situation like this
    happened in the future, how
    would you handle it?

Adapted from: Daniel Sonkin and Michael Durphy, *Learning To Live Without Violence.* San Francisco: Volcano Press, 1982.

application of the lessons being taught in the program. It also offers men a means for monitoring behavior and accessing their progress.

4. Reducing Stress

Stress also contributes to wife abuse, but its exact role is highly debated. Nevertheless, stress can be reduced and with it the anxiety that heightens anger making it difficult to communicate. Reducing the stress, as is the case with avoiding violence and communicating feelings, can, furthermore, help a man prove to himself that he can redirect his life, thereby encouraging him to work toward more substantial changes.

Some psychologists suggest that abusive behavior is merely a learned, albeit inappropriate, response to stress. If stress is reduced, violent behavior will lessen. But others contend that stress is merely a reinforcing rather than causal factor. In fact, some men who batter do not appear to be under any inordinate stress. Their predisposition for control is expressed in coercive action irrespective of stress. The violence, in this light, is more the result of social roles than psychological deficiency.

As suggested in Chapter 3, these two perceptions may complement one another, rather than be mutually exclusive. Many men aspire toward a sex role stereotype which they cannot fulfill. They are unable to live up to the masculine ideal instilled in them by their family, military experience, tough peers, and macho media images. They become worried about their shortcomings and experience stress.

More specifically, stress is an emotional and physiological response to a perceived threat, loss or change. It can be an event like being laid off from work, and the death of a loved one, or a situation like a boss who is uncooperative and a salary that is insufficient. In sum, an external matter appears out of one's control or disruptive to one's life. The mind and body in a sense are put on extra alert to compensate for the perceived threat. In doing double time, the body wears itself down as well as overreacts.

A portion of the men who batter have experienced recent stressful events that contribute directly to their abuse. As the event passes and the men readjust, the abuse subsides. However, the majority of abusers are more likely to suffer from chronic stress. For them, every event is stressful. Picking out a gift for a child's birthday, for instance, becomes a worrisome chore. These men obviously are more likely to be abusive, but their chronic stress in itself does not explain why they are violent particularly toward women, rather than coworkers, drinking friends, or a pet dog.

For some men, the chronic stress may be a diversion from deeper seated anxieties. They worry about expenses or their wife's fidelity to avoid having to face the existential dilemmas over which they have little control or which demand a change in them. The abuser is commonly insecure about his manhood and fears sexual impotency or sudden death. If chronic stress over petty issues is reduced, a man may therefore lapse into depression over personal shortcomings which come to the surface.

The deeper uncertainties often warrant a philosophical or spiritual search that goes beyond the counseling program. The men in a group session, however, can at least begin to talk about their common search for meaning and purpose in life. Some of their assumptions or doctrines, of course, are severely imposing and stressful. Consequently, they need to be rooted out. A frank talk along these lines can start men considering the place of theology in their lives and point them toward religious groups or writings that offer more constructive support.

There are four intermediate techniques that are widely used in helping men to specifically reduce their stress: guided imagery, relaxation exercises, positive self-talk, and changing patterns. All of these techniques can be practiced daily by individual group members as well as with a men's group at weekly meetings.

In *guided imagery*, group members are asked to envision a tranquil scene described by the counselor—a pastoral setting, an ocean beach, or a mountain valley (see Table 5-8). Ideally the

Table 5-8: Guided Imagery Exercise

"My Private Place: An Exercise in Creative Imagination"

Instructions to be read by counselor to clients: We'd like to share an exercise that may offer you an imaginary place to which you may retreat for relaxation and refreshment. Find a quiet, relaxing place, and give yourself enough uninterrupted time. You may choose to ask a friend to read the directions to you so you can close your eyes and let your imagination go. You could also tape record it and play it back to yourself.

Now, close your eyes and imagine that you are in your bedroom . . . see the entire room as clearly as possible . . . notice that a new door has appeared on one wall. The door has a doorknob. Approach it and put your hand on the knob noticing its texture and temperature . . . as you open the door, you find yourself in a new room, an addition to your house, a room that you've never seen before. The room is empty, except that it has several windows. Now, go inside and explore this room.

Now, you are going to begin to develop the environment in this room . . . where are the windows? Determine what views you would like to have out of each window (you might see an ocean from one, mountains from another) . . . now, furnish your room for yourself—including a special chair or pillow or couch on which you can rest and dream . . . you may want to add a work space, such as an art studio, a dance floor, or a writing desk. Make it happen immediately; be spontaneous; if you like music, listen for it or add a piano, guitar, flute and music stand. You might want to add elements of the outdoors into your room, such as an indoor waterfall, a tree or flora.

Be as creative and courageous as you can be. Remember, there are no limits. Now sit back and enjoy your private place . . . tell yourself that you can go to it to relax in the midst of a hassled day, to solve your problems, or to prepare yourself for sleep. The uses are as many and as varied as your needs. Have fun with it! When you are ready to return to the here-and-now, find a comfortable way to leave your private place, taking with you the feelings that you experienced there.

From: Regina Sara Ryan and John W. Tavris, *Wellness Workbook*. Berkeley, CA: Ten Speed Press, 1980, p. 143.

men in the group experience a peaceful feeling which can be regained by repeating the exercise individually.

Relaxation exercises are a means to become more aware of one's body tensions, and also to systematically release them. As a preliminary part of the exercise, the group members lie on the floor or sit in comfortable chairs, with their eyes closed. They are instructed to concentrate first on their breathing, then their pulse, and finally on different muscle groups (their head and shoulders, back and abdomen, lower body and legs). The men are then asked to describe the sensations they noticed. Was their breathing uneven and shallow? Were any muscles particularly tight?

To begin the relaxation exercise, the counselor instructs the men to assume a comfortable position with feet and legs uncrossed and hands resting lightly on their thighs or arms of chair. The counselor then softly offers the following directions:

Take five deep breaths holding each one to a count of five before releasing it. ("Inhale—one, . . . five—exhale.") Tighten as much as possible and then release completely various muscle groups starting at the head and shoulders and working down to the ankles and feet. ("Head and shoulders—tighten . . . release.") Clear your thoughts completely and repeat to yourself "I am relaxed," whenever a thought attempts to intrude. And after a minute or so of this meditation, gradually open your eyes. Compare your breathing, pulse and muscle sensations with your observations prior to the exercise.

Positive self-talk is a means of replacing worrisome and discouraging thoughts that may habitually intrude in one's thinking and cause stress. To learn positive self-talk, the men state or write the thoughts that come to mind in a stressful situation. "What do you think when your two children start arguing, begin to fight, and the phone rings?" Then, the men write assertions that specifically offset the negative thoughts. For example:

Negative Self-Talk: "Those darn kids are always causing trouble. They deserve whatever comes to them, they are so disagreeable! I ought to let both of them have it before they drive me crazy. Don't they ever think of anybody but themselves?''

Positive Self-Talk: ''I am feeling mad about all the commotion. However, I have the ability to respond creatively to this situation and resolve it. The children are capable of getting along and cooperating with me. I can remind them of that and talk with them about this particular disagreement. There is no need to feel pressured or lose my cool over this minor squabble that will pass in a few minutes anyhow.''

Lastly, men might be encouraged to *change some of the living patterns that perpetuate stress*. To help start this process, the men list on paper situations and events which have recently brought about stress. The counselor can offer some specific events—like the children doing poorly in school, disagreements with the in-laws over plans for a family reunion, or having to work overtime. He can suggest as well, daily routines that cause stress, such as gulping several cups of coffee in the morning, driving hurriedly to work, or watching late night TV (see Table 5-9). The men then check those items that bring the most stress. Finally, the group can discuss ways to change the situation. Would more contacts and friends help alleviate the stress? Would a hobby or sporting activity, a weekend vacation with the family or kids, or a heart-to-heart talk with the boss or co-workers be helpful?

5. Communicating Feelings

As studies indicate, the men who batter are relatively inexpressive and lack basic communications skills. As explained in Chapter 2, men in general are socialized to repress their feelings and disclose only essential information. The resulting self-containment helps men compete and accomplish tasks. By being ''tough,'' men can complete more work and maintain an edge on their competitor. However, this is often done at the expense of personal growth and others' well being.

Table 5-9: Dealing With Potential Stress

A Day In the Life of Joe and Roscoe

Potential Stress	Joe (Chronic Stress Pattern)	Roscoe (Healthy Stress Pattern)
Oversleeps—awakes at 7:30 instead of 6:30	**Action:** Gulps coffee, skips breakfast, cuts himself shaving, tears button off shirt getting dressed.	**Action:** Phones office to let them know he will be late. Eats a good breakfast.
	Thoughts: I can't be late again! The boss will be furious! I just know this is going to ruin my whole day.	**Thoughts:** No problem. I must have needed the extra sleep.
	Results: Leaves home anxious, worried, and hungry.	**Results:** Leaves home calm and relaxed.
Stuck behind slow driver	**Action:** Flashes lights, honks, grits teeth, curses, bangs on dashboard with fist. Finally passes on blind curve and nearly collides with oncoming car.	**Action:** Uses time to do relaxation exercises and to listen to his favorite radio station.
	Thought: What an idiot! Slow drivers should be put in jail! No consideration of others!	**Thoughts:** Here's a gift of time—how can I use it?
Staff meeting	**Action:** Sits in back, ignores speakers, and surreptitiously tries to work on monthly report.	**Action:** Listens carefully, and participates actively.
	Thoughts: What a waste of time. Who cares what's going on in all those other departments? I have more than I can handle keeping up with my own work.	**Thoughts:** It's really good to hear my co-workers' points of view. I can do my work a lot more effectively if I understand the big picture of what we're all trying to do.
	Results: Misses important input relating to his department. Is later reprimanded by superior.	**Results:** His supervisor compliments him on his suggestions.

Potential Stress	Joe (Chronic Stress Pattern)	Roscoe (Healthy Stress Pattern)
Noon—behind on desk work	**Action:** Skips lunch. Has coffee at desk. Spills coffee over important papers.	**Action:** Eats light lunch and goes for short walk in park.
	Thoughts: That's the last straw! Now I'll have to have this whole report typed over. I'll have to stay and work late.	**Thoughts:** I'll be in better shape for a good afternoon with a little exercise and some time out of the office.
Evening	**Action:** Arrives home 9 p.m. Family resentful. Ends up sleeping on couch. Does not fall asleep until long into the morning.	**Action:** Arrives home at usual time. Quiet evening with family. To bed by 11 p.m., falls asleep easily.
	Thoughts: What a life! If only I could run away and start over! It's just not worth it. I'll never amount to anything.	**Thoughts:** A good day! I felt really effective at work, and it was nice reading to the kids tonight.
	Results: Wakes up late again, feeling awful. Decides to call in sick.	**Results:** Wakes up early, feeling good.

From: Tom Ferguson, *Medical Self Care: Access to Health Fools.* New York: Summit Books, 1980.

Men carry this inexpressiveness, of course, into the home. Battered wives frequently complain that their husbands seldom talk about their feelings and have great difficulty in expressing their needs. If they do not receive what they want, they resort to coercion and outbursts. The women feel as if they are somehow supposed to read the man's mind—a difficult task when many of the men themselves do not understand their emotions and needs. When a woman responds with emotion, interestingly, men frequently dismiss it as being "hysterical." The woman's spurt of feeling resonates with the man's buried reservoir of emotion and threatens to bring it to the surface—a frightful prospect for one bent on maintaining control.

Therefore, helping men "get in touch" with their feelings is a vital step in group counseling. In the group interaction, the counselor can guide the men toward genuinely listening to one another, and affirming each other's contributions rather than talking over or being condescending to others. Also, the incident review, check-in's, and open-ended questionnaires provide a structured means of sharing feelings. Several other techniques can help develop expressiveness.

Men who batter need specific help in distinguishing their feelings from thoughts or observations. That is, a man may note that he feels like his wife is neglecting him. This is of course an accusation about another person rather than an expression of one's personal feelings. The real message may be, "I feel hurt when my wife does not speak to me after work." The men need, therefore, to learn to make "I feel . . ." disclosures that communicate how they personally feel. As they learn to do this, they are better able to communicate with their partners about their emotions and needs.

During group discussion, the counselor can remind the men to make genuine "I feel . . ." statements simply by inquiring, "But how did *you* feel?" Also, open-ended "I feel . . . " statements can pose hypothetical situations at home, at work, or in the meeting. For instance, a counselor might present the group with a list of questions such as:

When my wife tells me to get the lawn cut, I feel . . .

When my child leaves his or her room messy, I feel . . .

When my boss asks me to work overtime, I feel . . .

When the counselor interrupts and corrects me, I feel . . .

Several programs require the men to keep a daily log of "Feeling Statements." Each day the group members write down three feelings and the conditions that surrounded them to later present and discuss in a meeting. Besides noting their feelings, the men can outline three ways they might have expressed a particular feeling. For instance, if a man felt "hurt" because his child did not tell him that he or she lost a wallet, the man could have a) sobbed and pouted at the dinner table; b) told the child and wife that he felt hurt because they did not inform him about the matter; or c) conferred with a friend about the hurt, asking if he had ever had similar feelings. The counselor might simply inquire when each of the men felt happy, sad, hurt, satisfied, or afraid during the week, as part of the check-in of the meeting or during the course of the session.

Another objective in this regard is to help men develop more assertive, as opposed to aggressive, communication of their feelings (see Table 5-10). According to assertiveness training, our communication is either passive, assertive or aggressive. The most effective communication is generally the assertive form that explicitly expresses "I feel . . ." statements and their implications. The passive communicator withholds genuine feelings in a sense of impotence or fear; whereas, the aggressive communicator imposes them with accusations and coercion. Unfortunately, many men swing back and forth to extremes of passive and aggressive communication.

Similarly, Transactional Analysis (T.A.) outlines the range of an adult communicating to a "child" (aggressive and condescending), a child to parent (passive and dependent), or adult to adult (assertive and explicit). In terms of T.A., a man often

Table 5-10: Assertive Communication Training Model

Passive Communication—withholds emotions and deflects issues

"It's O.K., I really don't care." "Those sort of things just happen, I guess."
"It was probably my fault anyhow."

Assertive Communication—expresses feelings and explicitly identifies issues

"I feel angry about not being invited."
"I am happy that you came to talk with me about it."
"What you said hurts me very much."

Aggressive Communication—accuses others with generalizations

"You are basically a no-good creep."
"It's all your fault."
"If you hadn't been here it wouldn't have happened."

speaks to his wife as if she were a child, implying that he controls and directs her.

One final skill necessary for effective communication is knowing how to say "no." Many of the men who batter explain that they feel "put upon" by their families. The men insist that they do what their wives want them to do, but that they have to be violent to get their wives to do what they want. In part, the problem lies with a lack of assertiveness. Many of the men communicate their "no's" only with violent outbursts. Because "no" is often synonymous with being violent, some men passively hint about their dislikes or opposition to avoid the aggressive extreme; unfortunately with unsatisfying results.

Role playing may be used to let the men re-enact an incident that occurred during the week and to practice saying "no" in an assertive way. A man also can be presented with a hypothetical request from his wife, boss, clergy, child or relative to which he must respond in the negative. With each response, the man should first respond in a normal tone of voice, then in a loud tone of voice, and finally in a shouting tone of voice, in order to learn that he can be emphatic without being violent.

Of course, there are dangers that may accompany this new assertiveness. It may be misused to more effectively control one's wife. Furthermore, many of the "impositions" to which men learn to say "no" may be things that they should be doing. Therefore, the men need to be admonished: they have a right to express how they feel, but they do not have a right to expect their wives to conform to their feelings.

The new assertiveness, which can surprise as well as exploit women, can be moderated by putting men in role playing situations where they must assume the woman's role and respond to the assertive statements of a group member acting as a man. The individual assuming the role of the woman should kneel before the other man or sit on the floor while the other sits on a chair. The other group members note then, how the body posture and gestures of the individual acting as the husband become more severe as he escalates his "no" response. The other man assuming the role of the wife discusses his perceptions from the "subjected" position. This feedback can alert men to the implications of their body language. Often they bodily convey aggressive communication, even though they believe that their words are genuinely assertive.

6. Resolving Conflict

Most of the men who batter have learned that violence is the most expedient way to resolve conflict. They, therefore, need to develop alternative problem solving skills. There are some precautions, once again, that must be heeded in equipping men with additional tools. Learning alternatives to violence should not be a means to more clever manipulation. Many men simply need to learn the art of compromise and concession. That is, many of their problems can be solved by giving up some power rather than expecting to get one's own way. However threatening the prospect, making some compromises will be more beneficial than continuing abuses which eventually drive away one's family.

The men who batter are schooled in the "bigger hammer" approach to problem solving, which compounds their difficulties rather than eases them. If something does not fit in place, they simply reach for a bigger hammer and swing harder until they force a fit. In their minds, they are expected to be tough, get things done, and use force. In fact, to not be at least occasionally violent is, according to some men, a sign of weakness. Violence, particularly against women, is tolerable and even necessary. It is a man's privilege and duty to keep women in their place. Consequently, even the men who consciously want to stop their violence against women "automatically" react violently to problems.

However, reaching a compromise can entail vigorous negotiation and perhaps a non-physical fight. The men may benefit, therefore, from learning just how to carry on such a "fight." This may begin with teaching them the rules for fair fighting (see Table 5-11) and practicing them in a role play with the group. One of the group members acting as the wife attempts to press the other man acting as the husband into breaking the rules. The counselor and other members serve as judges scoring the husband for each rule he violates.

Other techniques to teach men conflict resolution might include: problem solving exercises, role playing and group consultation. Problem solving exercises provide practice in analyzing personal situations (see Table 5-12). Too often, the men who batter do not analyze a situation but rather lunge ahead impulsively. This exercise prompts men to instead access the components of a problem and develop a suitable strategy by following problem solving procedures as outlined in the steps below:

1.   Select an immediate problem and define it in concrete terms

2.   Identify its component parts

3. Set a series of goals that correspond to at least one of the components

4. Generate alternative ways to reach it

5. Evaluate each alternative

6. Select the best one

7. Outline the steps to implement their strategy

At a subsequent session, the men should report on their action and, if necessary, obtain group advisement to readjust their strategy.

For instance, a man is angry over his children's disobedience. He might define the problem, "My oldest daughter does not do the chores when I ask her to." The component parts of the problem might include a) she refuses to do the dishes without help from her brother; b) she has forgotten to take out the trash; and c) she says that she has straightened her room but it is only partially cleaned. The most immediate goal might be to get her to follow through on what she agrees to do. The alternatives might be a) that the man discuss thoroughly with his daughter, while sitting together at the kitchen table, how he feels about her behavior and how she feels about his reactions to it; b) that he post a schedule of chores and some consequences if they are not fulfilled; c) that he offer to help with some chores or have the other child specifically assigned to some; and d) that he ask the daughter to propose a way to get the work done and then try her plan for at least two weeks.

Role playing can also be adapted to assist with this objective. A man might be asked to demonstrate in front of the group his plan of action derived in the problem solving exercise. In this way, he not only practices his action, but can also receive coaching from the observing group members. Also, the counselor can turn incidents recounted during the check-in into a role play by asking "What would you like to say to your wife about this? Address me as if I were her." The counselor in turn responds as if he were

Table 5-11: Rules for Fair Fighting
(or How to Have an Argument With Your Partner
and Remain Friends)

Introduction: These lists were completed at a group meeting of men at RAVEN on December 17, 1980. We don't think that this is the last word on how to have a fight, especially when women did not help directly with the list. We do believe, however, that this is a very good start. See if your men's group can make a comparable listing or improve on this one.

Fair Behavior

- Speaking one at a time and allowing equal time
- Looking for compromises
- Trying not to generalize
- Allowing for time-outs and breathers (see notes)
- Observing rules that you set
- No forcing/No hitting or threats
- Showing personal respect
- Being honest with yourself and them
- Giving your reasons
- Admitting when you are wrong
- Making your understandings clear by repeating them and writing them down

Unfair Behavior

- Name calling
- Opening old wounds/dredging up the past
- Getting off on tangents
- Intimidation/threats of violence
- Changing the rules and not saying so
- Expecting there to be a winner and a loser
- Saving up gripes to dump all at once
- Reading the others' mind
- Denying the facts
- Using sex as a leverage
- Gloating over a "victory"
- Appearing to ignore the other

Notes: A breather or time-out means that you go have a cigarette or a cup of tea for about a half hour and then *return* to finish the discussion.

We noticed that many of the unfair behaviors are stuff we learned as kids against other kids and our parents. "Growing up" is part of learning fair rules.

From: RAVEN, St. Louis, MO.

Table 5-12: Problem Solving Exercise

Directions: Select one problem that has recently been bothering you and respond to each of the following steps with that problem in mind.

1. Define the problem:

2. Identify its components:
   a)
   b)
   c)
   d)

3. Set a specific goal you would like to accomplish:

4. Generate alternative means for reaching that goal:
   a)
   b)
   c)
   d)

5. Evaluate each alternative:
   a)
   b)
   c)
   d)

6. Select the best solution:

7. Outline specific steps to implement your solution (when, where, how, etc.):

8. Take action and evaluate it:

9. Redefine problem (and repeat steps if necessary):

the wife and instigates a hypothetical dialogue for others in the group to evaluate. At the conclusion, the man might repeat the exchange, incorporating the advice of the observers.

Lastly, the incident review can serve as a springboard for group consultation. After an individual reviews a recent "close call," the counselor should request group members to offer suggestions, comments, or observations. Inevitably, someone in the group has been in a similar situation. He can recount what he did to avoid violence. Others can speculate on how the problem might have been handled. In this way, the group session can evolve into a problem solving workshop with the group members posing problems encountered during the week and receiving possible solutions. Along the way, the group can break the discussion to test out a solution through a role play. During the week, the "buddy" phone calls can encourage and evaluate the implementation.

7. Undoing Sex Role Stereotypes

An essential objective of group counseling is to educate men to the sex role dynamics that sanction and perpetuate violence against women. The men who batter must be helped to see how, at the "micro-level" of society, they are socialized by their family, peers, work place, media, and clubs to dominate women. They must also be helped to recognize the discrimination at the "micro-level"—that is, how our social structures and institutions systematically exclude women and elevate men.

As feminists in particular have observed, wife abuse is a consequence of sex role stereotypes. Men are socialized to be in charge of women, treat them as sex objects, and subject them to abuse and violence. Furthermore, men have a privileged position within the social structure. They inflict violence unintentionally or purposefully in order to maintain their wealth, status, and power. A sexist ideology develops to justify this patriarchy. Amidst this oppression, many women adopt a false consciousness in which they believe themselves to be inferior as the sexism suggests.

A variety of aides, therefore, needs to be employed for "consciousness raising," such as women speakers, films on abuse, language exercises, macro-analysis diagrams, and charts of household duties. These aides are much preferred to a counselor's effort to discuss or explain sexism. The men in a self-help group are likely to resist or oppose the counselor who lectures as an authority on women. The aides allow the counselor to act more as a broker soliciting the men's feelings and helping the men deal with them.

Women are the best educators of sexism, since they have been the recipients of it. A staff member of a shelter, women lawyer, a battered woman, or rape victim can help confront a group of men with the realities of sexism. The women need only relate their experiences growing up, dealing with marriage, and succeeding in a profession to impart some decisive lessons. The women's personal accounts of abuse or harassment are often the first time men have heard what it is like to be on the receiving end of their behavior. Their battered wives or rape victims are seldom in a position to confront them as these women are. In many mixed sessions, the men spontaneously ask "what if's" that help them understand the woman's perspective. There are also a number of films and articles which effectively expose sex role stereotypes (see Appendix).

Regardless of the medium, it is essential that the counselor spend as much time debriefing as was spent in the presentation. The presentations inevitably evoke reactions that the men too often repress and add to their anger. The counselor can help air these feelings by starting with a "check-in" immediately after the talk, film, or reading: "How are you feeling right now?" The task is to keep the conversation at the affective rather than cognitive level, and help the men develop some empathy for the woman's situation. The tendency, however, is to drift into intellectualizing that explains away the issues and keeps the men at arm's length.

Language exercises are a convenient means to expose the subtleties of socialization (see Table 5-13). The group members are asked to recall expressions associated with women and then men, or slang terms for the male genitals, female genitals, and the act of intercourse. After a substantial list has been established on a chalkboard or wall chart, the group assesses the implications of each list. Inevitably the slang for men's genitals is weapon-like ("tool," "thing," "dick") and the terms for women's genitals are soft, animal-like receptacles (pussey," "hole," "hair pie"). The words for intercourse are impersonal and aggressive ("do it," "jam," "screw"). The implication is that sex is something that men impose on women, rather than an intimate relationship of caring feelings. The group members should discuss, then, how they learned to objectify women and its effect on their behavior (see especially Jack Litewka, "The Socialized Penis," in Shapiro and Shapiro, eds.. 1979).

Macro-analysis diagrams can help men recognize the connections between social structures and interpersonal behavior (see Table 5-14). The counselor writes a particular behavior—such as "wife abuse"—in the center of a chalkboard or large piece of paper. The group members then record in a ring around the specified behavior any values, norms and sanctions that contribute to this behavior. The names of social groups, institutions, or organizations that contribute to this inner ring of reinforcement are recorded in the next outer ring. As they develop the diagram, the men connect the different items with arrows until an interlocking web of causal vectors is drawn.

A charting of household tasks brings the broad abstractions of macro-analysis into personal view. Each group member identifies the chores that various family members did that day (or week) to reveal the women's inordinate responsibility for the home. The

Table 5-13: Common Expressions
Associated With Women(Language Exercise)

Instructions: Group members are asked to offer common expressions used to describe women or some other aspects of gender. After a list has been compiled and written on a chalk board or wall chart, the group should discuss the implications of language. Its derogatory portrayal of women should be apparent. Why do these negative images prevail and how do they influence men's treatment of women?

cover girl
unwed mother
little old lady
hen pecking
chick
my little chickadee
she's a perfect little lady
that's not ladylike
a bevy of beauties
wine, women, and song
don't worry your pretty little head
isn't she cute?
pretty little maids all in a row
loose woman
slut, tramp, two bit whore
party doll
be a good girl
Mother Goose
my little princess
girl talk
dumb broad
dumb blond
silly woman
gentleman prefer blonds
blonds have more fun
air head, space head
just a housewife
she's ugly but she sure can cook
a woman's work is never done
keep her barefoot and pregnant
knocked up
the little woman
Jewish mother
plain Jane
wall flower
a girl in every port
a woman's place is in the home
stand by your man

virgin, spinster, old maid
nothing like a dame
gal Friday
just like a woman
you women don't know what you want
you can never understand a woman
dizzy dame
flighty
telephone, telegraph, tell a woman
earth mother
woman driver
she goes all the way
what a piece of ...
playmate of the month
what a pair of ...
red hot mama
girl watching
sex pot
girlie magazine
find 'em, feel 'em,...
flat as a board
boy, is she stacked
what a pair of legs
foxy lady
she's a dog bitch
she's no spring chicken
daddy's little girl
mommy's little helper
ladies first
hysterical female
she's so cute when she's mad
she's really bright for a woman
you've come a long way baby
old bag
playboy bunny
does she or doesn't she?
mother hen

men might similarly be asked to list what they have specifically done for their wife and vice versa within the last week. The counselor may have to prompt the group by asking who cleaned the dishes, picked up the children, paid the bills, etc. In discussing the results, the men realize the women's vast support and hopefully develop a greater appreciation for their wives' contributions—and for their wives themselves.

8. Taking Social Action

Ultimately, men who batter need to change their self-image. They need to see themselves not as masculine creatures prone toward anger and violence, but as self-directed individuals capable of empathy and gentleness. Such a change of course, is seldom achieved within an 8-12 week span of sessions. The new self-image of a changing man needs to be furthered or sustained through social action.

Most of the men who do significantly change experience a kind of "conversion." In the conversion process, the program becomes the man's alter ego. The men begin to identify with the program staff and volunteers more than their former acquaintances. They eventually become "true believers" proclaiming the program's benefits to newcomers. Similar to a religious conversion, the "converts" see themselves saved by some force beyond themselves and "witness" to its impact with praise and thankfulness (see Fagan et al., 1983:65). Likewise, the reformed batterers can become overzealous, and want more responsibility than they may be able to handle.

This process serves to reinforce and affirm the changes taking place. The men feel the momentum of the program supporting them. It is no longer an individual against his problems but many changing men working together. The new identification gives the former batterers something to live up to—it gives them a sense of purpose and importance, too.

Table 5-14: Macro-Analysis Diagram

Instructions: The diagram below was constructed by a group of men in the RAVEN program in an effort to illustrate some of interrelated causes of wife abuse. Have your group select this or a similar social problem, "brainstorm" a series of causes, and discuss their relationship.

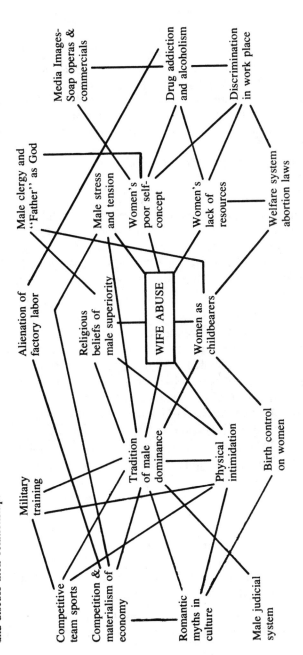

From: RAVEN, St. Louis, MO.

The men appear to develop a new sense of self-esteem when they begin to do something for someone else. Even a simple gesture can move a man's mind off his own problems and self-pity. The men learn to give of themselves rather than "take," as they do in their accustomed positions of power. They also realize in the helping process that they can affect a change in their surroundings. They need not be a victim of circumstance but can make things better for others and themselves.

The men might be simply assigned to perform a helping task during the week and report on the action at the following week's meeting. A group member might be asked to assist another individual in the group. He could drive someone to a job interview, help tune a car or repair a faucet. Or, he might be encouraged to volunteer in a social service program for the elderly or handicapped.

The men's movement outward needs to continue one step further, however. The men can learn, also, to "help" change the institutions and organizations that contribute to their stress and reinforce their violence. To begin, the men might visit at least one meeting of a social action coalition in their area—anything from a nuclear freeze meeting, local NOW chapter, to unemployed workers committee. They can report to their group what they learned from the social action meeting. Ideally, they will observe that individuals can join together to make significant social changes.

Another possibility is for the men to become a contributing part of the men's program rather than just a recipient of its services. They can begin by attending business meetings, potluck suppers, training sessions, conferences, and retreats. The men can take a further step by serving as a public speaker on abuse at churches, service clubs, or union meetings. By telling their story to others, they again affirm to themselves their change and also provide an example for other men. They, moreover, extend the arms of the program further into the community.

Ideally, the men might gain the confidence and knowledge to organize a social action group of their own. They might begin by organizing former program participants for follow-up meetings. They could plan to do promotion in their own neighborhood or develop a support group at their work place. The men in such a group might select an institution on their macro-analysis diagram (see Table 5-14) and use their problem solving skills (see Table 5-12) to develop a plan to change it. The social action can be as immediate as challenging fellow workers at the lunch table about their sexist language and lewd jokes or as broad scale as launching a campaign to raise funds for a shelter or child care program.

6

Programing for
Social Change

Wife abuse, as suggested at the outset, is ultimately a social problem. To unearth its deep roots, we must therefore "treat" society as well as reform individual abusers. Supervised self-help programs for men can contribute to some larger social change, but realistically their efforts reap minimal results from the massive field of men in need of change. The programs must, therefore, be a part of some larger movement for change—one that extends at least to the community, if not to society at large.

This chapter considers this tall but necessary order. It begins with a reflection on the limitations that face even the most ambitious men's programs. There are, however, some fronts on which programs can launch, or sustain, a movement for change. Three of these possibilities are outlined. One is the institutional training in which volunteers and staff of men's and women's programs train other social service staffs to respond more effectively to wife abuse. Two, school curriculum can be expanded or revised to more decisively teach children about sex role stereotypes and their consequences. Three, building a coalition that more genuinely includes the grassroots can allow for the dialogue, as well as the energy, to forge ahead in new directions.

The Shortcomings of Social Service

Group counseling for men who batter is a necessary response to wife abuse, albeit not a sufficient one. As argued in Chapter 1, many battered women return to their batterers, or the batterers move on to other victims. Therefore, the perpetrator of the violence—the man—must be dealt with to insure more security for the victims. Moreover, it is recommended that men help men change their abusive behavior. Most abusers are tremendously resistant to conventional psychotherapy and the feminist perspective—in part because these directly implicate the men. Male counselors can serve to bridge the perceptions of the batterer and the demands of therapy and feminism. Ideally, the men's groups can lead the batterer out of himself and toward social action.

Researchers and activists alike, nevertheless, urge "treating" the social roots of wife abuse—in particular, by educating the community to the nature of abuse and addressing the institutions that foster it. Most programs, however, have barely enough funding to maintain their service activities, let alone develop community-based components to prevent abuse. Consequently, most efforts are relegated to promotional talks to community groups and college classes, primarily with the intent of raising financial support for their services. In reality, the prospects are limited for organizing neighborhood groups, retraining social workers, sensitizing police, instructing clergy, empowering young women, resocializing young men, or developing family care activities.

Moreover, even the best programs for men who batter reach a scant few. RAVEN, for instance, estimates that it has assisted about 550 of the 100,000 persistent abusers in the St. Louis area. Less than half of those who contact the program complete it and become non-violent. Also, the burnout rate of those working with abusers (child abusers, rapists, wife abusers, etc.) is particularly high—as much as 50% a year (Star, 1982). Yet the incidence of abuse continues to rise, especially with current increases in unemployment. More men are home with their families, suffering stress from economic hardship and a blow to their self-esteem from the loss of their status as breadwinner.

Consequently, helping men who batter may have to be viewed as putting money in the bank. You have to make a lot of saves before you begin to get a return. The more men who are helped, the more men who batter are going to come forward. But frequently we become so preoccupied with increasing the balance that we fail to reinvest it in more productive options. In other words, countering the centripetal force that besets most social service endeavors is not an easy task. The funds are scarce, staffing limited, and the direction outward uncharted. It is all many programs can do to stay alive.

Institutional Training

The number of existing men's and women's programs is miniscule in comparison to the job to be done. Therefore, especially in these times of limited social action, it may be a practical measure to enlist available allies as well as shore up the ranks. Despite recent severe cutbacks in social services, there remain a number of viable agency staff and professionals dealing with related problems, like drug and alcohol abuse, child welfare, divorce proceedings, and so on. Granted, the past oversight of many social agencies has made women's shelters and men's self-help groups necessary. Nevertheless, these services can share some of the responsibility for helping the batterer, if made aware of the issues and processes. In this effort, the more independent alternative programs would be free to devote more time to community education. The men's programs, for instance, could work more on meeting the last two counseling objectives outlined in the previous chapter—undoing sex role stereotypes and taking social action.

In essence, participants in the men's program—staff, volunteers, and group members—can work to change institutions and make them more responsive to the issues of wife abuse and less likely to be one of the social factors reinforcing it. They can discuss with clergy, mental health workers, police, doctors, lawyers, and judges—most of whom are men—their perceptions of domestic violence and perhaps in the process, expose their unwitting accessory to the problem. Simply communicating the experience of men who batter and the need to be responsible for the part men play in domestic violence is a start.

This can be accomplished through talks, workshops, and local conferences requiring minimal costs and organization. The men's program staff could visit a church board meeting, ministerial association luncheon, police staff briefing, mental health board gathering, or a business club dinner. Representatives from a number of service institutions might be invited for a lunch together or to a potluck business meeting of program staff and participants. The coordination and referral among services is likely to improve through these informal linkages. Eventually, domestic violence teams could be established to formally coordinate a variety of services addressing wife abuse.

Men's self-help programs are also in an ideal position to work with the police. The program staff and the police have much in common—their socialization as men and concern about wife abuse. Police, in particular, are concerned about the batterers whom they repeatedly face on domestic violence calls. The police feel there is little they can do with the men. A viable men's program, therefore, serves the police's interests and in turn the police can perhaps help meet some of the program's needs. The men's program staff might form workshops on domestic violence for patrol police, have police attend various group sessions, accompany police on domestic violence calls, or make follow-up inquiries to abusers.

The fundamental assumption behind these proposals is that a variety of men have to work together, not only to address the social dimensions of wife abuse, but also to make a men's program work. Too often the responsibility of helping men who batter is left to a few. In fact, it is frequently passed off to the women activists, in part, because women are perceived as being the most affected by the problem and have the natural nurturing skills to assist the abusers.

Furthermore, men are reluctant to come forward and genuinely get involved with their "brothers" as women have done with their "sisters." Men have obviously something to gain in tolerating wife abuse. As one staff member of a program for men who batter notes: ". . . Men who rape or batter do the dirty work for (other men); they are the terrorists whose acts keep the entire population of women in fear and in line" (Adams, 1982). A few dedicated male counselors servicing men who batter, in this light, buy time for other men. Therefore, the services must eventually turn outward to "treat" all men and the patriarchy which they perpetuate, if wife abuse is to be undone.

Consequently, the more successful anti-sexist programs, like EMERGE in Boston, devote as much effort to developing a collectivity of men as they do to counseling batterers. Their aim is to involve a variety of men working cooperatively to bring about change in themselves and the society around them. Their organization provides, in the process, an example for other services and a force to be reckoned with, as well as services for men in need of support.

Revamping School Curriculum

The most available and important audience for community education may be the students who are conveniently assembled in our schools. So-called primary treatment is best directed toward them, because they are still in the midst of a socialization process that predisposes men to violence against women. Interestingly, a variety of studies indicate that the incidence as well as tolerance of abuse actually increases rather than decreases with higher education. It may be that the competitive norms and cognitive emphasis of formal education, itself, contribute to the preponderance of domestic violence.

Most shelters and men's programs are already active in the schools. In most cases, however, the occasional invitations to give school talks are the result of personal contact rather than a systematic plan. One teacher or another is personally concerned about wife abuse—perhaps he or she has a friend who has been battered—and, therefore, invites a shelter staff member to address his or her class. Some schools have introduced courses in marriage and the family or sex education classes that consider the problem of domestic violence. These courses offer a convenient open door for program staff to more regularly present workshops for students. However, education on wife abuse should ultimately become an established part of the curriculum like drug and alcohol education and health and physical education. The extent and severity of wife abuse warrant some systematic warning and prevention.

At the elementary school level, more "affective" learning which specifically addresses sex role stereotypes is in order. In the back-to-basics-movement, much of the humanistic education designed to explore students' feelings and individuality has been pushed aside. The boys continue to be encouraged into competitive sports and mathematics (see Hartley, 1974). Girls have made more progress in asserting themselves on the playground and in the classroom than boys have in diversifying their interests and behavior. However, girls remain behind the boys in overall achievement test scores principally because of sex role differences (see Tavris and Offir, 1977).

The media, more than ever, bombards children with stereotypic images. Both families and schools have to teach children to decode media messages, especially those received from the six hours a day of T.V. they watch. The children can begin simply by identifying the sex roles represented in their classroom textbooks. Who is the hero of the story—a male or female? How many occupations are represented for the males—for the females? Can a female be a truck driver or a carpenter, too? In a systematic survey of 2,750 children's stories, the Women-on-Words-and-Images research group found the ratio of boy-centered to girl-centered stories to be 5:2 and tallied 147 occupations for boys and 26 for girls (cited in Tavris and Offir, 1977:177-179). Cartoon shows, T.V. commercials, and movies like *Star Wars* can similarly be evaluated and questioned. What of the incidents fights, car rammings, and murders seen on weekly television programs? A child sees as many as 18,000 murders on television by the time he or she is eighteen years of age.

At the secondary level, there need to be courses on family relations that specifically alert students to wife abuse and that train them in assertive communication and conflict resolution. Many of the exercises outlined in Chapter 5 can easily be adpated to the classroom for these purposes. Students also have to be alerted to the sophisticated advertising and films that exploit their emerging sexuality to make money. Again, the students need help in decoding magazine ads and film images, so that they can make conscious choices about the roles which they accept for themselves. A simple tabulation of the roles of men and women in print or T.V. advertisements, including the voice-over announcements, will reveal women in a subservient, dependent, or silly role four to one over men. The "Marlboro Man" and the "Endless Summer" heroine portray an image of independence, but without revealing the high cost to personal relationships.

It is also very important for the differences in employment opportunity to be exposed. Most high school females feel that sufficient changes have been brought about through the women's movement allowing them to be and do what they want. The facts, of course, speak against the myth of the "new women." Of the twenty-three million women in the business world, twenty million are secretaries (there were only four million secretaries in 1950), and the average earnings of women (less than 60% of men's) have been falling further behind their male counterparts. Furthermore, only 18% of American scientists, 8% of the engineers, and 4% of our nation's legislators are women. Closer to home, how many women are among our towns' political and business leaders? What do these statistics imply about who controls the wealth, power, and status in our society (see Table 6-1).

How should students respond to sex role stereotypes in their own lives? Can a woman afford to be independent, assertive, or ambitious if she marries a traditional man? What if she wants to work and he does not want her to? What if he wants more children and she does not? Male and female students, in confronting such questions together, expose the blindness of romance and gain insights into the realities of marriage. Not only can the content of these questions be revealing, but so can the interaction in obtaining the answers. In discussing hypothetical relationship contracts (see Table 6-2) does the male press for his own way, set up conditions, or vaguely shrug his shoulders only to rebel when his limit is reached? Is his communication passive, aggressive or assertive? The interaction patterns may be a hint of what is to come in the marriage relationship (see also Table 6-3 for a guide to more cooperative relationships).

At the college level, the general education curriculum should require courses in family issues and social change. Such courses need, however, to be presented more as an interactive workshop than a lecture series. Again, the students can be prompted to evaluate their predilections toward control and violence through many of the exercises presented in the previous chapters. They can discuss their feelings and views with one another, and more deeply explore themselves through keeping journals. Unfortunately, in elective courses of this topic and format, more women enroll than men—four times as many.

By sophomore year, the "lughead" syndrome has claimed many of the men. They have their eyes set firmly on a place in business and will compete ruthlessly to get there. If they are successful in this "man's world," they expect to be rewarded with, among other things, the best looking women. Even in college, the most prestigious fraternities and toughest athletes get the best "dames." The male students, in other words, already are in the driver's seat and are reluctant to give it up.

The entrenchment of this traditional male role may be in part responsible for the startling incidence of abuse on campuses. In one survey of undergraduates at St. John's University in Minnesota, 21.2% of the freshman and sophomores had been abused or had

Table 6-1: Sexism in the Economy

Males Control the Economy

Worldwide

Women perform nearly two thirds of the world's work hours, yet comprise only one third of the official workforce. Men receive 90% of the world's income and own 99% of all property.

News & Views of Federally Employed Women,
November-December, 1980

In the USA: Women Business Owners

In 1979, 411 thousand women managed their own business, compared with 1.4 million men. Most women's businesses were in personal and business services, or in retail trade.

U.S. Department of Labor, Women's Bureau, 1979

In the USA: Women on Corporate Boards

Women represent only 1.8% of total corporate board membership.

New York Times, April 22, 1981

Women as Corporation Directors

There are fewer than 300 women among the 15,000 directors of the 1,300 largest corporations in the U.S.

WEECN News, Fall, 1979

Women Managers

Of all companies which reported to the EEOC in 1978, women were 40% of employees but 17% of managers and officials. Minority women were only 3% of managers, compared to 15% of white men, 7% of white women and 7% of minority men. Women managers dominate the less well-paying slots, such as office managers and retail sales managers. In 1977 the median wage of women managers was $10,203 compared to $18,704 for men. Of persons earning over $25,000, under 4% were women.

U.S. Department of Labor, Women's Bureau, 1979

Banks

In 1975 the Council on Economic Priorities found that while 63% of all bank employees were women, only 5% of them held middle-management posts, and less than 1% held top-executive jobs. Senator Proxmire, of the Senate Banking Committee, said that there is no new information since 1975 to make him temper his belief that banking is, "the most discriminating, prejudiced business in the world."

The Civil Rights Quarterly, Perspectives, October, 1981

The Results of Male Control

Normal Is Male

"Norms of work life have developed to fit the uninterrupted—the male—career. Women cannot match this pattern, because they interrupt work life to bare children and to care for them . . . . Women's work lives proceed at a different rhythm from men's. They are marked by interruptions for pregnancy, maternity, and child care. In a world of work fashioned and fitted to men, these interruptions handicap women in finding jobs, retraining, and being considered for promotion, that is, for the rewards presumably attractive in economic life."—says Professor Alice Cook of Cornell University.

Status of Women in the Labor Force: August 1981

Women were 43.2% of the total civilian labor force. 52.4% of all women were in the labor force.

Bureau of Labor Statistics, August, 1981

Median Income of All People Over 15 Years, by Sex and Race, 1980	All Males	$12,530	All Females	$4,920
	White Males	13,328	White Females	4,947
	Black Males	8,790	Black Females	4,580
	Hispanic Males	9,659	Hispanic Females	4,405
	U.S. Department of Commerce, 1981			

Median Income of All People Over 15 Years, Working Full Time, Year-Round, by Sex and Race, 1980	All Males	$19,173	All Females	$11,591
	White Males	19,720	White Females	11,703
	Black Males	13,875	Black Females	10,915
	Hispanic Males	13,790	Hispanic Females	9,887
	U.S. Department of Commerce, 1981			

Median Family Income, 1980	Married couple with wife in labor force	$26,879
	Married couple with wife not in labor force	18,972
	Male householder, no wife present	17,519
	Female householder, no husband present	10,408
	U.S. Department of Commerce, 1981	

Woman-Headed Families

In 1980, 15% of families were headed by women. These families made up half of all poor families.

U.S. Department of Commerce, 1981

Wage Gap in 24 Jobs

Comparisons in 24 Occupations

	1980 Median Weekly Earnings		Women's Pay as Percentage of Men's
	Women	Men	
Postal clerks	$347	$359	97%
Nurses, dietitians, therapists	$292	$305	96%
Health technicians	$253	$299	85%
Textile workers	$175	$206	85%
Secondary school teachers	$290	$347	84%
Social workers	$263	$322	82%
College teachers	$349	$448	78%
Food-service workers	$138	$176	78%
Computer specialists	$335	$439	76%
Lawyers	$397	$532	75%
Editors, reporters	$286	$389	74%
Scientists	$325	$455	71%
Accountants	$277	$400	69%
Cashiers	$149	$216	69%
Engineers	$348	$503	69%
Assemblers	$186	$272	68%
Office-machine operators	$201	$296	68%
Bookkeepers	$203	$306	66%
Factory inspectors	$204	$314	65%
Office managers	$255	$392	65%
Retail-sales clerks	$140	$216	65%
Insurance agents, brokers	$238	$379	63%
Bank officials financial managers	$270	$472	57%
Retail-sales managers	$195	$348	56%

U.S. News & World Report, June 22, 1981

From: *Fact Sheets on Institutional Sexism.* Council on Interracial Books for Children, 1841 Broadway, New York, NY 10023; January, 1982.

Table 6-2: Relationship Contract

Name: Should the wife take on the husband's last name, the husband take on the wife's name, both take on a hyphenated name, both a new name, or both keep their names? If there are children, what will their surname be?

Birth Control: What kind? Whose responsibility?

Household Duties: Who does what?

Leisure Time: Should evenings and weekends be spent together? Who decides what to do? Should vacations be spent together? With children? Separately?

Living Arrangements: Where will the couple live? What kind of privacy do you want? Shared bedroom? Do you want to live with others? What will you and your partner do if you want to live in different places because of jobs, or for any other reason?

Money: Will both partners be wage earners? If so, will you pool your income or each keep own salary? Share equally the cost of living expenses and keep the remainder for yourselves? Who will pay the bills and keep account of the budget?

Sexual Rights: Are both partners committed to monogamy? Who initiates sex? Is either partner free not to respond?

Children: How many? When? What about adoption? Who will take primary responsibility for raising the children? Will one partner have to quit a job?

Other Relationships: Are you and your partner free to make relationships with other people? With those of the same sex? With those of the opposite sex? What is to be the extent of these relationships? Do you include each other in these relationships?

From: Eleanor Morrison and Mila Underhill Price, *Values in Sexuality: A New Approach to Sex Education.* New York: Hart Publishers, 1974.

Table 6-3: Guidelines for Promoting an Equal Man-Woman Relationship

1 . Be completely honest; that means not keeping secrets from each other as well as talking straight.

2 . Ask for what you want 100% of the time. Trust that you and your partner can negotiate an acceptable cooperative agreement and both get a high percentage of what you want with each other.

3 . Be conscious of sex roles, experiment with reversing them, and then end them entirely.

4 . Be conscious of competition and power plays. Be equals who cooperate so that both win as much as possible.

5 . Be equal in sexual responsibility and in orgasmic satisfaction.

6 . Have friends, especially of your own sex, for support and in order to develop a loving sense of yourself as a man or woman by seeing and identifying with the beauty of persons of your own sex and then in yourself.

7 . Have privacy for yourself, that is, be with yourself (as opposed to being "alone") in order to know yourself well and to be in good communication with your center and your own sense of who you are and what you want in life.

8 . Have inside yourself a ready willing and able "Nurturing Parent" to support, nurture, and protect your own self-creation and the struggles between you and your partner.

9 . Don't demand or expect perfection from yourself or another human being. Be understanding of human error as a necessary part of growth and allow yourself and others time and space to grow in.

10 . Don't make each other into commodities by trying to own or possess another in the service of your own insecurity. Allow yourself and your partner as much freedom as you can.

From: RAVEN, St. Louis, MO.

inflicted abuse in premarital relationships at least once. As many as four percent of the abused indicated that they had been struck with closed fists (cited in *Response*, July/August, 1981).

The student counseling services are in the best position to address these problems. They might establish a supervised self-help program, as outlined in this book, to help some of the men. Residential counselors can organize men's groups in dormitories and fraternities to discuss the relationship problems compounded by male socialization. The stress, impotency, alcoholism, heart ailments, and mid-life crisis are all related to the male sex role stereotype (Goldberg, 1976) and can provide grist for informal group meetings.

Approaching abuse through the treatment of alcoholism may get more of the college abusers to come forward, because many college men can admit more readily to the drinking that affects them directly than to the abuse that injures others. The heavy drinking relieves inhibition and stress associated with the traditional masculinity, but encourages much of the abuse, rape, and harrassment that occurs on campus. Men's awareness can also be prompted by a men's group of non-batterers which meets to discuss common concerns and develop alternative role models. A course in "Men and Masculinity" addressing some of the readings listed in the Appendix would also add to the visibility of men's issues.

But to affect the broader student population, male dominance of the institution, itself, must be addressed. The non-academic activities outside the classroom may be more powerful educators than the class lectures and counseling. If not, they certainly offer a confusing contradiction to the professions of teachers. The dramatic gender differences demonstrated in collegiate sports, choice of major, the Greek fraternities, and the staffing of the university, for instance, serve to maintain the patriarchy.

In response, some universities have diligently instituted women's studies programs, women's counseling services, and recruitment of women faculty and deans. Unfortunately, the accomplishments in this regard have been limited, because of the entrenched male administrations and contracting budgets. A few universities have reformed the structure of student residences to improve social relationships. The Committee on Undergraduate Residential Life (C.U.R.L.) at Princeton University, for instance, recently established a residential college system in which groups of men and women live in the same complex for four years, sharing social activities as well as dining together. The "colleges" also provide trips to cultural events in New York City and weekend outings. Faculty sponsors join in informal college socializing and college sponsored seminars. The aim is to promote an atmosphere outside the fraternity-like clubs that is less cliquish, competitive, and sexist.

Building a Coalition

There is much a men's program can do to shore up its own ranks and intensify the work being done to reform batterers. Men's programs specifically can do more to include women in their program efforts, increase the participation of minorities, and develop men's centers or residential facilities. Each of these inclusions might not only add greater numbers to the work with men, but will also serve to advance our understanding of wife abuse.

Women in Men's Programs

An all male program does have practical advantages. Namely, it has an easier time attracting men who batter and encouraging them to take responsibility for their behavior. Nevertheless, it needs the direction that only women can offer, in order to counter the potential competition between men's and women's services and to keep the men alert to the central issues. As mentioned, the masculine tendency for avoidance, denial, intellectualizing, task orientation, control, and power can undermine the good intentions of the best men's group.

While there is question in many circles about the role of men in women's shelters, there are also questions about women serving as counselors in programs for men who batter. As discussed in Chapter 1, the adjunct men's programs of women's shelters allow for great flexibility as well as assure cooperation. Such an arrangement allows for more convenient counseling of couples, mixed groups, or single-sex groups. But as mentioned, this model may receive a limited number of self-referrals from apprehensive men. Also, the boundary lines between men's and women's programs can no doubt be adjusted to accommodate the strengths of the various staffs, the resources of each program, and the needs of the men who batter. The shelter might offer support groups for the wives of the batterers in the men's program, or the men's program could sponsor such a group employing women staff. The men's program might, furthermore, invite women from the shelter to attend group sessions or maintain a staff member to participate in the groups and check-up periodically on the men's wives.

There are also many able women counselors who have demonstrated their effectiveness in leading abuser groups and who have in fact started abuser programs themselves (see, for instance, Ganley, 1981; Garnet and Moss, 1982). This book endorses men serving as lead counselors for all men groups, but does not mean to preclude the possibility of female counselors for men. The abuser's defenses and transference are likely to intensify with a woman counselor, but the woman counselor may be more alert to the subtler male tendencies of intellectualizing and power plays. She can offer, most importantly, a woman's perspective that can help men who batter become appreciative of their partners and women in general.

Including Minorities

Moreover, if the men's programs are going to make an impact, they must also build a coalition with Black, Hispanic, Native American, and Asian communities. These "People of Color" have been noticeably underrepresented in women's shelters as well as men's programs. Although there is a significant incidence of physical abuse among low income minorities, only a small percentage of these social groups use shelter facilities and men's programs, or serve as program staff and volunteers.

Some researchers indicate that the incidence of physical abuse is greater among low income minorities (Pelton, 1978; Cazenave and Straus, in press). The implication, they insist, is that structural poverty is a significant factor in abuse and must be treated rather than psychological deficiencies. Cazenave and Straus (in press) found, however, that black family violence was less common than white family violence in a national survey. Moreover, Davis (1981) suggests that the myth of black abusers is another manifestation of white society's attempt to establish blacks as bestial and inferior, and thereby justify its harsh treatment of them.

Social workers note that racial minorities are caught in a double bind of wife abuse and racial discrimination. The struggle for survival makes abuse merely one of several miseries and, therefore, less likely to evoke a decisive response. The women especially carry the burden of their sex and their color. They may be, consequently, more reluctant to counter a man who appears a victim himself of the racial discrimination of white society (see especially Hooks, 1981; Moraga and Anzaldua, eds., 1981; Wallace, 1978).

The people of color, therefore, have a unique perspective on the underside of society, and this perspective could help to broaden the base and effectiveness of men's and women's programs. As victims of racial and sexual oppression, people of color are the most familiar with the flaws of our social institutions and class structure. "It's like putting society under a huge magnifying glass," a black counselor once explained of his experience. In order to discuss this perspective and articulate it, men of color need to be associated with a men's program. This requires the obvious step of actively accommodating them. Employing minority counselors, promoting minority participation in conferences and training sessions, and assuring a critical mass of minority participants in

group sessions as the EMERGE program has been doing, is a start
in this direction.

The specific role of minorities, as well as former batterers,
in men's programs is, nevertheless, debated between social service and social action proponents. On the one hand, the social service orientation suggests that programs will gradually expand and
become more extensive and effective, as we learn more and train
better. It is a sufficient challenge just to assist the receptive middle
and working class abusers, let alone those individuals with
problems compounded by poverty and discrimination. On the other
hand, the social action orientation would suggest that services are
typically staffed by whites and are middle class in value orientation. Consequently, minorities feel isolated, even ostracized, and
removed from their supportive kin. The treatment programs,
moreover, do little to address the racial oppression and chronic
unemployment that affect minority abusers. "Talk like us, act like
us, think like us—and you'll be O.K." is their misleading message.
The men's programs, therefore, appear to be just another exten-
sion of the white paternalism that preserves the status quo.

Proponents of both orientations, nevertheless, desire more
minority participation but are constrained increasingly by practical
limitations. The demands of survival or more substantial
opportunities draw away potential minority volunteers or staff.
Contracting budgets limit the funding needed to support a diverse
staff. Moreover, pressures to professionalize limit the participation of volunteers and former batterers.

There is, however, some recourse to this inertia. The counseling services and community education can be developed in unison
but not separately. Many trained counselors are not sufficiently
familiar with the neighborhood networks to organize men into
support groups, mobilize them for social action, or even to recruit
them for counseling groups. Minority volunteers and former
batterers can work particularly within their neighborhoods to alert
others to the possibilities of change. Without at least this sort of
inclusion, the number of men joining men's programs is not likely

to increase substantially and the impact of the program will be minimized.

Forming Men's Centers

As the base of support broadens, men may eventually be able to expand their services to include a residential component. Residential men's centers do have some practical advantages. One, they can provide an atmosphere that more decisively challenges the abuser's sense of isolation and more comprehensively monitors his behavior. Two, a residential men's center offers a place to "cool off" for men encountered by police on domestic violence calls. Three, such centers present an alternative to battered women being uprooted from the convenience of their homes and children being removed from their friends and schools. The centers would allow for the perpetrator of the violence to be relocated or confined rather than the victim who has already suffered enough.

Such a center could particularly assist police in one of their principal concerns: what are they to do about the men who batter? Police frequently complain that they have no place to put abusers. Consequently, the men often end up in a bar, causing fights, or driving recklessly. The police are left with no recourse but to encourage the battered women to leave the house for a shelter.

The men's center might offer some men a more substantial form of "time-out" (see Table 5-6). Most men presently do not seek help until they are personally desperate or are forced to do so. However, as a "climate of acceptance" develops, more men may seek prevention of their violence against women. They may accept a place to "cool off" free from the conditions that may set them off again.

Furthermore, a men's center could give men a way-station in the midst of their transition. It would more substantially counter the sense of isolation and depression that besets men who batter during the long week between group sessions. Most men are likely to disclose themselves and unravel their fears in a less structured, more informal setting—one the center could no doubt create. The center also presents greater security, since the constant supervision could more systematically monitor abusers' alcohol use and tempers.

A residential facility for men need not require the overhead nor space of a women's shelter. A church basement, YMCA wing, or a vacated home would be sufficient to house a barracks-like arrangement of bunk beds, bath facility, and meeting room. Former batterers could do the remodeling necessary for the center and assist with the night supervision and maintenance of the facility. This constructive activity, in itself, could help foster a spirit of purpose and unity needed by many changing men.

The challenges facing such a center, of course, need also to be considered. For one thing, a residential facility might severely compete for resources with the existing women's shelters. However, if coordinated properly with the shelter, the men's center could ease the shelter's overflow by removing some of the men from their homes. Secondly, such a facility could easily become a haven for "deviants" avoiding responsibility and justifying one another's abuse. The center, therefore, would need a decisive set of regulations establishing the conditions of the men's stay. If men did not conform to the regulations and attend required group sessions, they could be dismissed from the facility and referred to the jail for housing. The center consequently would have to be closely coordinated with law enforcement agencies to assure this necessary leverage.

A third concern would be that the men's center would be questioned by social action proponents. Can a facility run for men by men be trusted to maintain its commitment to feminist ideals and not become merely a self-serving project for men? Just as shelters have occasionally been criticized as being "breeding grounds" for anti-men sentiments, the men's centers could easily reinforce the male tendency for "blaming the victim." There is, unfortunately, justification for this concern even in the self-help groups.

A men's center could offer some consolations, however, to the social action proponents, as well as to the social service advocates. It does represent a mobilization of men involved in change and presents an alternative to the sexist professional services. The center would no doubt require a broad base of active support from men at large which could merge in a collective effort with staff, volunteers, and participants sharing in the decision-making process and implementation of the program. It could demonstrate, in this way, that men can cooperatively work to change themselves and other men. Thus, it would present an alternative institution to the community—a visible symbol of men in change. Moreover, the men's center could form the basis for community education and support groups for men in change. Amidst the stark patriarchy of the day, some havens for changing men may be at least a temporary necessity.

A Final Note:
A Movement Toward The New Man

As argued throughout this book, counseling in itself is not enough. There are social roots to wife abuse that must be addressed. While social service is presently humane and necessary, it has in the past led to cooptation (see Sullivan, 1982; Schechtner, 1982; Dobash and Dobash, 1981; Piven and Cloward, 1976). Despite good intentions, service programs become preoccupied with their own survival and neglect community education. Their vision is compromised for broader acceptance and support. As they gain greater respectability, they lose their capacity to agitate for change. Yet, greater appeal is paradoxically an ingredient in building a coalition for change.

It is important to understand, therefore, that the cooptation is induced as much from without as from within. The institutions, which social action advocates most seek to change, neutralize the challenge by accommodating or reshaping the social change efforts. They require more organization and more professionalism, which leads to more exclusiveness in programs and dependence from "clients." This cooptation gets society off the hook, so to speak, and focuses attention on the abusers and abused. Wife abuse, for example, is increasingly being identified less as a social problem and more as a psychological problem. Behaviorist treatments proliferate in academic journals on family issues. In addition, more and more women's and men's programs are turning into adjuncts to mainstream mental health programs.·

This is not to dismiss the contributions of the social service emphasis, but to question its escalating momentum and expansion. How, especialy in these conservative times, do we insure social activists their rightful place? How do we keep batterers moving toward substantial change in themselves as well as in society?

In our crisis-oriented society, a new issue frequently eclipses a current one, diverting community support from emerging programs. The focus in many communities is already shifting from women's shelters to services for unemployed workers. Consequently, the advocates who wish to stop wife abuse suffer further emotional and financial strain. The day-to-day confrontation with violence and entrenched sexism is depleting in itself. A program can easily appear as a small beachhead facing a tidal wave. As suggested, a step toward revival may be to develop a network of support and encouragement with allied workers and program participants. Ironically, some professional support and more community involvement can also be of some aid in making programs viable.

To shore up the beachhead, it may be helpful to start with the ultimate objective rather than to continually postpone it. Attending more to the destination can make charting the way to get there easier. Men's programs are ultimately working toward establishing a new form of manhood. But what shape is this new ideal to take? Do they want men to be non-violent, gentle, cooperative, nurturing, and sensitive? Is some sort of androgyny desired in which the male and female attributes are encouraged simultaneously? Need the new man run the risk of being insecure, emasculated, or whimpy—or perhaps self-pitying and self-indulgent? Obviously, the objective needs to be articulated and discussed more completely; it also needs to be kept free of an ideological straight jacket that would shape people into what they are not.

The feminist movement, with its diversity of voices, has helped to surface the feminine side of humanity, historically so repressed and feared by men. In the process of alerting women to the strength of their feminine nature, the women's movement has also alerted some men to their feminine natures. Carl Jung, in particular, insisted that male and female are psychologically androgynous— that is, they both have potential to express feminine and masculine qualities (see Sanford, 1980). Men, consequently, in this new social climate, are beginning to seek out their capacity for gentleness, nurturance, cooperation, intuitiveness, and healing.

It is not only that some individual men have resonated with the women's movement and experimented with the social changes, it has thrust upon them. Increasingly, changing men are resonating with other changing men. Consequently, a men's movement, however factionalized, has emerged, and media stars like Alan Alda and Phil Donahue suggest to the public at large that men can at least be sensitive and concerned.

The groundswell is admittedly difficult to access. The momentum of the men's movement has slowed along with the temporary stall in the women's movement. The current tight economy has forced some changing men back into the foray of intense competition. The severe backlash of the right wing against those questioning the *status quo* has also had its toll. Furthermore, books like *Real Men Don't Eat Quiche* have propagandized the macho stronghold.

Nevertheless, in quiet and unobtrusive ways, men continue to change. I recall my own turn from making war models and playing college football and rugby, to practicing pacificism as a conscientious objector and counseling in programs for men who batter.

I think of a former academic colleague and now close friend who has gone through similar changes. Steve was brought up in a military family and served as a demolition officer in Vietnam; now he works as a househusband chauffering his two daughters to and from their after school activities, preparing dinner for his wife and children, and cleaning their house, while doing volunteer work for several environmental groups. Rich comes to mind too. He had a childhood of being abused by an alcoholic father, 17 years in the steel mills, and two failed marriages. A few years ago, he sought out a men's program, stopped abusing his own family, and now volunteers to work with other men of similar backgrounds. I could no doubt fill this book with male acquaintances like these who are building a new image of man.

This new image of man, however ill-defined, can motivate and reinforce the efforts of men in change. It can remind us in these hard times of what is possible and give us the strength to be it. The new man may in fact be an inevitability rather than an ideal. Amidst the intense conflicts among family members, different ethnic and minority groups, and the nations of the world, it is becoming increasingly clear that some radical reconceptions are in order. We ultimately need to change our conceptions of ourselves and relationship to one another.

Putting on the "new man," moreover, can be a satisfaction in itself. It allows us to be more expressive, responsive, versatile, and innovative—qualities increasingly at a premium in the post-industrial society. Furthermore, the new man is freeing—not only from the confinements of male socialization, but also from the burdens of being an oppressor.

In sum, rather than deaden the movements for change, the tumult of the times may be refining them. The popularity and security of the "old man" may in fact be shaken loose, and the "old man" may fall of his own dead weight. The best way to help our brothers through this social upheaval—especially men who batter—may be through our active demonstration of this "new man." In this way we will not only be helping them, but helping ourselves.

Appendix

Resources

Books: Wife Abuse

Armstrong, Louise, *The Home Front: Notes from the Family War Zone*. New York: McGraw Hill, 1983.
An examination of the "tradition" of abuse that is part of our society, forcefully arguing it be treated not sympathetically by psychologists, but decisively as a criminal act.

Borkowski, Margaret, Mervyn Murch, and Val Walker, *Marital Violence: The Community Response*. New York: Tavistock, 1983.
An examination of the shortcomings in government policy and social services dealing with domestic violence—and recommendations to improve services available for battered women.

Davidson, Terry, *Conjugal Crime: Understanding and Changing the Wife Abuse Problem*. New York: Hawthorn, 1978.
A discussion of the historical, cultural, and interpersonal aspects of wife abuse.

Dobash, R. Emerson, and Russell Dobash, *Violence Against Wives*. New York: The Free Press, 1979.
A compelling treatment of the link between patriarchy and wife abuse urging an "action-oriented" response to the issue of power.

Finkelhor, D., R. Gelles, G. Hotaling, and M. Straus (eds.), *The Dark Side of Families: Current Family Violence Research*. 1983.
A collection of prominent research articles on a wide range of abuse issues pressing toward some theoretical understanding of abuse.

Giles-Sims, Jean, *Wife Battering: A Systems Theory Approach*. New York: Guilford Press, 1983.
A longitudinal study of abused women revealing the web of relationships sustaining the destructive partnership.

Hofeller, Kathleen, *Battered Women, Shattered Lives*. Saratoga, CA: R & E Publishers, 1983.
Presents practical advice for dealing with abuse including guidelines for starting women's programs and traits common to abusers.

Langley, Roger and Richard Levy, *Wife Beating: The Silent Crisis*. New York: Pocket Books, 1977.
An earlier expose integrating a variety of case histories into a call for new social services.

Martin, Del, *Battered Wives*. New York: Pocket Books, 1976.
The founding classic reviewing the nature of wife abuse and society's feeble response to it.

McEvoy, A.W., and J.B. Brookings. *Helping Battered Women: A Volunteer's Handbook for Assisting Victims of Marital Violence*. Holmes Beach, FL: Learning Publications, Inc., 1982.
A practical guide for volunteers and professionals who work with battered women, especially in shelter programming.

Pagelow, Mildred Daley, *Woman-Battering: Victims and Their Experiences*. Beverly Hills, CA: Sage Publications, 1981.
A quantitative and qualitative study of shelter residents supporting social learning and sociopolitical theories of abuse.

Roberts, Albert, (ed.), *Battered Women and Their Families: Intervention Strategies and Treatment Programs*. New York: Springer, 1984.
A collection of papers that examine current issues in program development and techniques for working with battered women, abusive men, and their children.

Rouse, Linda P. *You Are Not Alone: A Guide for Battered Women*. Holmes Beach, FL: Learning Publications, Inc., 1985. (Also available in abridged booklet.)
This down-to-earth guide helps battered women assess the likelihood of the batterer changing, as well as offers suggestions for improving the quality of their lives.

Roy, Maria (ed.), *Battered Women: A Psychosociological Study of Domestic Violence*. New York: Van Nostrand Reinhold, 1977.
A collection of research and treatment articles with a section devoted to law enforcement practices.

Roy, Maria (ed.), *The Abusive Partner: An Analysis of Domestic Battering*. New York: Van Nostrand Reinhold, 1982.
An offering of articles on treatment programs for special populations of men who batter.

Schechter, Susan, *Women and Male Violence: The Visions and Struggles of the Battered Women's Movement*. Boston: South End Press, 1982.
A radical critique of the theory, research, and treatment of wife abuse with designs for maintaining a grassroots response to wife abuse.

Stacey, William, and Anson Shupe, *The Family Secret: Domestic Violence in America*. Boston: Beacon, 1983.
A readable study of abused women in the Dallas area which focuses on women's options and the impact on all family members.

Straus, Murray, Richard Gelles, and Suzanne Steinmetz, *Behind Closed Doors: Violence in the American Family*. New York: Anchor/Doubleday, 1980.
A national survey that surfaces the extent of violence in American families and suggests mutual aggression between partners is a problem.

Walker, Lenore, *The Battered Women*. New York: Harper, 1979.
A vivid clinical study of abused women offering a typology of the kinds of abuse and the notion of the violence cycle.

Books: Men's Roles

Beneke, Timothy, *Men on Rape: What They Have To Say About Sexual Violence.*
New York: St. Martin's, 1982.
A series of interviews with men who have raped and with police, lawyers, counselors and women who have dealt with rape cases.

David, Deborah, and Robert Brannon (ed.), *The Forty-Nine Percent Majority*, *2nd ed.* Reading, MA: Addison-Wesley, 1982.
An anthology of strong essays on the male sex role.

Ehrenreich, Barbara, *The Hearts of Men: American Dreams and the Flight from Commitment.* Garden City, NY: Anchor/Doubleday, 1983.
A reconsideration of the past twenty years of cultural history revealing the change in male attitudes to be responsible for the breakdown in the family—not women's liberation.

Farrell, Warren, *The Liberated Man.* New York: Random House, 1974.
A founding appeal for more expressiveness, feeling and care in men.

Fasteau, Marc, *The Male Machine.* New York: Delta, 1974.
A compelling discussion of the compulsive and imposing role men assume in American society.

Gerzon, Mark, *A Choice of Heroes: The Changing Faces of American Manhood.*
New York: Houghton-Mifflin, 1983.
A personal and historical critique of the prevailing images of manhood and the emerging roles for the new man.

Kiley, Dan, *The Peter Pan Principle: Men Who Have Never Grown Up.* New York: Dodd-Mead, 1983.
A popularized account of men's emotional dependencies and the problems they cause in relationships.

Lewis, Robert (ed.), *Men in Difficult Times.* Englewood Cliffs, NJ: Prentice Hall, 1981.
A collection of articles, essays, and poetry highlighting the personal changes going on in men.

Nichols, Jack, *Men's Liberation: A New Definition of Masculinity.* New York: Penguin, 1974.
Another of the initial critiques on the male sex role urging a reconception of men's lives.

Pleck, Joseph, and Jack Sawyer (eds.), *Men and Masculinity.* New York: Prentice-Hall, 1974.
A varied group of essays on men and their relationships to women, children, work, and other men.

Pleck, Joseph, *The Myth of Masculinity*. Cambridge, MA: MIT Press, 1981. An analysis of research on the male sex role and revised assessment of its implications pinpointing the social basis of gender (includes bibliography of "Male Role Studies").

Rubin, Lillian, *Intimate Strangers: Men and Women Together*. New York: Harper & Row, 1983. An engaging discussion of the difficulties men and women encounter in their relationships largely due to sex role socialization.

Shapiro, Evelyn, and Barry Shapiro (eds.), *The Women Say/The Men Say: The Women's Liberation Movement and Men's Consciousness*. New York: Delta, 1979. A wide range of excerpts and articles addressing personal and political dimensions of marriage, manhood, battering, rape, the work place, and so on.

Snodgrass, Jon (ed.), *For Men Against Sexism*. New York: Times Charge Press, 1977. A collection of poignant writings on changing men and their response to patriarchy.

Films

A Family Affair,VISCOM Productions, 1047 Shipple Ave., Redwood City, CA 94063 (28 min.) Documentary drama follows family from battering incident to police action and court proceedings.

An Acquired Taste, New Day Films, P.O. Box 315, Franklin Lakes, NJ 07417 (26 min.) A 40-year-old filmmaker's wry look at the school, work, and media influences that shaped his life and exposes in particular the American obsession with being "number one."

Battered Women: Violence Behind Closed Doors, MTI Teleprograms, 3710 Commercial Ave., Northbrook, IL 60062 (24 min.) Discussion by battered women (and some men who batter) of the fear and helplessness associated with abuse.

Between Men (Masculinity and the Military), United Documentary Films, P.O. Box 315, Franklin Lakes, NJ 07417 (57 min.) A stunning documentary of the impact of military experience on men's personal lives.

Domestic Violence: The All-American Crime, Task Force on Battered Women, 1228 W. Mitchel St., Milwaukee, WI 53204 (30 min.)
Explores the root causes of domestic violence in cultural attitudes and historical violence.

Family Violence in America: The Conspiracy of Violence, FMS Productions, 1777 N. Vine St., Los Angeles, CA 90028 (30 min.)
A broad look at victims, abusers, lawyers, service directors, and experts considering the nature of domestic violence and how to break its cycle.

Growing Up Gay, King Entertainment, 235 East 45 St., New York, NY 10017 (30 min. videotape)
A sensitive documentary about four very different young people and their reflections on being a homosexual in contemporary America.

Heroes and Strangers, New Day Films, P.O. Box 315, Franklin Lakes, NJ 07417 (25 min.)
In frank conversations adult sons and daughters discuss their family relationships with their fathers and reflect on its impact on their lives.

Men's Lives, New Day Films, P.O. Box 315, Franklin Lakes, NJ 07417 (44 min.)
A reflection on growing up as a male and the socialization processes that influence us in the process.

New Relations: A Film About Fathers and Sons, Plainsong Productions, 47 Halifax St., Jamaica Plains, MA 02130 (30 min.)
A documentary of challenges and questions faced by an excepting father and an introduction to changing sex roles and different parenting styles.

The Other Side of Rape, Health Services Consortium, 103 Laurel Ave., Carrboro, NC 27510 (30 min. videotape)
A reenactment of a rape scene and treatment of the victim to evoke feelings and discussion.

Time Out Series: Deck the Halls, Up the Creek, Shifting Gears, ODN Productions, 74 Varick St., New York, NY 10013 (44 min.)
Three short dramatizations of violent incidents to stimulate discussion and self-examination.

To Have and To Hold, New Day Films, P.O. Box 315, Franklin Lakes, NJ 07417 (25 min.)
The first documentary examining the problem of abuse from the man's experience of it.

We Will Not Be Beaten, Transition House Films, 120 Boylston St., #708, Boston, MA 02116 (B & W, 35 min.)
Produced by women in battering relationships about their determination to escape battering despite society's neglect.

Why Men Rape, Learning Corp. of America, 1350 Ave. of Americas, New York, NY 10019 (40 min.)
Interviews with a variety of convicted rapists on their motivation to rape and underlying power needs.

Self-Help Books For Men

Bach, George, and Peter Wyden, *The Intimate Enemy: How to Fight Fair in Love in Marriage*. New York: Avon, 1981.

Benson, Herbert, and Miriam Klipper, *Relaxation Response*. New York: Avon, 1976.

Gaylin, William, *Feelings: Our Vital Signs*. New York: Ballantine, 1980.

Goldberg, Herb, *The New Male-Female Relationship*. New York: Signet, 1983.

Julty, Sam, *Men's Bodies, Men's Selves*. New York: Delta, 1983.

Lieberman, Mendel, and Marion Hardie, *Resolving Family and Other Conflicts: Everybody Wins*. Santa Cruz, CA: Unity Press, 1982.

Rosen, Gerald, *The Relaxation Book: An Illustrated Self-Help Program*. New York: Prentice-Hall, 1977.

Ryan, Regina Sara, and John Travis, *Wellness Workbook: A Guide to Attaining High Level Wellness*. Berkeley, CA: Ten Speed Press, 1980.

Selye, Hans, *Stress Without Distress*. New York: Signet, 1975.

Walters, Richard, *Anger-Yours, Mine, and What To Do About It*. Grand Rapids, MI: Zondervan, 1981.

Zibergeld, Bernard, *Male Sexuality: A Guide to Sexual Fulfillment*. Boston: Little Brown, 1978.

Manuals From Men Who Batter Programs

Batterers Anonymous Manual, 1980, The Coalitions for Prevention of Abuse Against Women and Children, P.O. Box 29, Redlands, CA 92373 ($8).
A brief outline of the format and procedure for setting up a Batterers Anonymous Program including press releases.

Confronting the Batterer: A Guidebook to Creating the Spouse Abuse Educational Workshop, 1983, by Phyllis Frank and Beverly Houghton, Volunteer Counseling Service, 151 S. Main St., New City, NY 10956 ($15).
Outlines a short-term educational program for men who batter modeled on a DWI program focusing on teaching legal and social consequences of battering.

Court-Mandated Counseling for Men Who Batter: A Three Day Workshop for Mental Health Professionals, Participants Manual, 1981, by Ann Gangley, Center for Women Policy Studies, 2000 P St., N.W., Suite 508, Washington, DC 20036 ($10).
A review of topics important to court referral program including intake procedure, assessment, and some basic treatment activities.

Cracking the Corporations: Finding Corporate Funding for Family Violence Programs, 1981, by Margaret Dunkle, Center for Women Policy Studies, 2000 P St., N.W., Suite 508, Washington, DC 20036 ($5).
A guide to fundraising for grass-roots and non-profit organizations including a bibliography on corporate giving and Foundation Center's references.

Helping The Abuser: Intervening Effectively in Family Violence, 1983, by Barbara Star, Family Services Association of America, 44 E. 23rd St., New York, NY 10010 ($20).
A book of profiles of programs for child abusers, sex offenders, and one chapter on men who batter their wives, including a summary of treatment procedures.

Learning to Live Without Violence: A Handbook for Men, 1982, by Dan Sonkin and Michael Durphy, Volcano Press, Dept. B., 330 Ellis St., San Francisco, CA 94102 ($10).
A workbook of weekly assignments and exercises for dealing with anger, stress, inexpressiveness, non-assertive communication, and drinking.

Organizing and Implementing Services for Men Who Batter, 1980, by EMERGE, 25 Huntington Ave., Boston, MA 02116 ($25).
Explains assumptions, policies and guidelines for a cooperatively managed anti-sexist organization for men who batter. EMERGE, in Boston, is one of the founding men's programs.

The Hitting Habit: Anger Control For Battering Couples, 1984, by Jeanne Deschner, The Free Press, New York, NY ($19).
A book setting forth a treatment for individual couples and couples' groups which psychologically addresses spouse and child abuse.

Wife Abuse in the Armed Forces, 1981, by Lois West, W. Turner and Ellen Dunwoody, Center for Women Policy Studies, 2000 P St., N.W., Suite 508, Washington, DC 20036 ($10).
A monograph examining wife abuse in the military and the military social service programs to deal with it.

Periodicals

Aegis: Magazine on Ending Violence Against Women, Feminist Alliance Against Rape, P.O. Box 21033, Washington, DC 20009
A forum for activists examining the root causes of violence against women and strategy to end it.

Brother: The News Quarterly of the National Men's Organization c/o Regional Youth Adult Project, 330 Ellis, St., Room 506, San Francisco, CA 94102.
An extensive newsletter of short articles, reviews, resources, and issues related to a movement of changing men (includes task force on violence against women).

Changing Men's Bookshelf c/o Food for Thought Books, 67 N. Pleasant St., Amherst, MA 01002.
Offers a bibliography and mail order for books on men's issues.

Fact Sheet on Institutional Sexism, 1982, Council on Interracial Books for Children, 1841 Broadway, New York, NY 10023.
A booklet of comparing men's and women's status in a variety of fields—politics, education, religion, employment, etc.

Machomania, SAM Project, University YMCA, 1001 South Wright St., Champaign, IL 61820.
An occasional newsletter of writings from participants in abuser programs and their reflections on their violence and efforts to stop it.

M: Gentle Men for Gender Justice, 306 N. Brooks St., Madison, WI 53715.
Quarterly publication of poetry, stories, news pieces and articles forwarding androgynous change in men.

Network News, c/o RAVEN, 6665 Delmar, Room 301, St. Louis, MO 63130.
A quarterly exchange of photocopied ideas, concerns and resource materials submitted by staff from several different programs for men who batter.

Response (to the victimization of women and children), Center for Women Policy Studies, 2000 P St., N.W., Suite 508, Washington, DC 20036.
A quarterly professional journal reviewing research, books, programs, and legislation in the field of domestic violence and sexual assault.

Victimology: An International Journal, Victimology, Inc., 2333 N. Vernon Street, Arlington, VA, 22207.
A journal of academic articles on the dynamics of victimization from a variety of disciplines.

Resource Centers

Center for Women Policy Studies, 2000 P St., N.W., Suite 508, Washington, DC 20036.
A national clearinghouse for information, manuals, legislation related to domestic violence and publisher of the RESPONSE journal.

Family Resource Center, Dept. of Sociology, University of New Hampshire, Durham, NH 03824.
Bibliography of academic studies and research methodology related to the family.

Military Family Resource Center, Toll-free phone number 800-336-4592.
Provides technical assistance and general information for those working with military families experiencing family problems.

National Clearinghouse on Marital Rape, Women's History Research Center, 2325 Oak St., Berkeley, CA 94708.
Includes access to newsletters, reports, and bibliographies on issues of marital rape so often a part of wife abuse.

National Coalition Against Domestic Violence, c/o 1500 Massachusetts Ave., N.W., Suite 35, Washington, DC 20036.
A network of women's shelter programs with a feminist orientation and concerns for abuser programs.

NOTE: The majority of states have statewide coalitions or networks of organizations working against domestic violence which are responsible for public education, lobbying, and fund disbursement.

Programs For Men Who Batter

AMEND (Greater Denver Area)
P.O. Box 385
Commerce City, CO 80037

AWAIC—Men's Counseling Program
P.O. Box 6086
Wyomissing, PA 19610

Batterer's Anonymous
c/o The Coalition for the Prevention of Abuse of Women and Children
P.O. Box 29
Redlands, CA 92373

Batterers Program
House of Ruth
P.O. Box 7276
Baltimore, MD 21218

BRAVO
Mid Missouri Men's Resource Group
Route 1, Box 276E
Ashland, MO 65010

Domestic Abuse Intervention Project
2 East 5 St.
Duluth, MN 55805

Domestic Abuse Project
2445 Park Ave., South
Minneapolis, MN 55404

Domestic Assault Project
V.A. Medical Center
Tacoma, WA 98493

Domestic Violence Project, Inc.
684 Cloverdale Ave.
Ann Arbor, MI 48105

EMERGE
25 Huntington Ave., Room 324
Boston, MA 02116

Family Diversion Network
2001 Chicon
Austin, TX 78722

Marin Abused Women's Services
Men's Program
1717 Fifth Ave.
San Rafael, CA 94901

MEN (Men Emerging Now)
211 4th St., Room 304
Juneau, AK 99801

Men Against Domestic Violence
YMCA
52 Howe St.
New Haven, CT 06511

Men for Nonviolence
1122 Broadway
Fort Wayne, IN 46802

Men Stopping Violence
1307 Iverson St.
Atlanta, GA 30307

Men's Counseling Program
405 Broadway
Tacoma, WA 98402

The Men's Project
c/o Westport Allen Center
706 W. 42nd St.
Kansas City, MO 64111

MOVE
3004 16th St., Room 112
San Francisco, CA 94103

Project RAP
Family Service of Philadelphia
311 S. Juniper St.
Philadelphia, PA 19107

RAVEN (Rape and Violence End Now)
Craig Norberg, Program Coordinator
6665 Delmar, Suite 302
St. Louis, MO 63130

Second Step
726 Wood St.
Pittsburgh, PA 15221

Therapy for Abusive Behavior
c/o Good Neighbors Unlimited
271 Thelma Ave.
Glen Burnie, MD 21061

NOTE: For more extensive listings, see "Programs for Men Who Batter: Parts I and II," in *Response*, April and June, 1980; "Programs Offering Services for Men Who Batter," in EMERGE Manual, 1981; "Directory of Respondents to National Survey of Services for Batterers," Appendix in Maria Roy, *Abusive Partner*, 1982; "Subscriber Listing," in *Network News*, RAVEN, St. Louis, MO.

References

Adams, David, "Women Batterers: The Sins of Our Brothers." *Sojourner: The New England Women's Journal.* (May), 1982.

Adams, David, and Andrew McCormick, "Men Unlearning Violence: A Group Approach Based on the Collective Model." In Roy (ed.), *The Abusive Partner.* New York: Van Nostrand Reinhold, 1982.

Adams, David, and Isidore Penn, "Men in Groups: The Socialization and Resocialization of Men Who Batter." Paper presented at the annual meeting of the American Orthopsychiatric Association, April, 1981.

Armstrong, Louise, *The Home Front: Notes From the Family War Zone.* New York: McGraw Hill, 1983.

Bach, George, and Peter Wyden, *The Intimate Enemy.* New York: Avon, 1981.

Bagarozzi, Dennis, and C. Winter Giddings, "Conjugal Violence: A Critical Review of Current Research and Clinical Practices." *The American Journal of Family Therapy,* 11:1:3-15, 1983.

Ball-Rokeach, S.J., "Normative and Deviant Violence From a Conflict Perspective." *Social Problems.* 28:45-62, 1980.

Bandura, Albert, *Aggression: A Social Learning Analysis.* Englewood Cliffs, NJ: Prentice-Hall, 1973.

Benke, Timothy, *Men on Rape: What They Have To Say About Sexual Violence.* New York: St. Martin's Press, 1982.

Benson, Herbert, and Miriam Klipper, *Relaxation Response.* New York: Avon, 1976.

Berkowitz, Leonard, "The Goals of Aggression." In Finkelhor et al. (eds.), *The Dark Side of Families.* Beverly Hills, CA: Sage Publishers, 1983.

Berkowitz, Leonard, "Is Criminal Violence Normative Behavior: Hostile and Instrumental Aggression in Violent Incidents." *Journal of Research in Crime and Delinquency.* (July): 148-161, 1979.

Bern, Elliot, "From Violent Incident to Spouse Abuse Syndrome." *Social Casework.* 63:1 (Jan):3-12, 1982.

Blumenthal, M., R. Kahn, F. Andrews, and K. Head, *Justifying Violence: Attitudes and American Men*. Ann Arbor, MI: Institute for Social Research, University of Michigan, 1972.

Borkowski, M, M. Murch, and V. Walker, *Marital Violence: The Community Response*. New York: Tavistock, 1983.

Bowker, Lee, *Beating Wife-Beating*. Lexington, MA: Lexington Books, 1983a.

Bowker, Lee, "Marital Rape: A Distinct Syndrome?" *Social Casework*. 64:6 (June): 347-352, 1983b.

Bowker, Lee, and Kristine MacCallum, "Demolishing Myths About Wife-Beating." Paper presented at the Tenth World Congress of Sociology, Research Committee on Sociology of Deviance and Social Control, 1982.

Boyd, V. D., "Domestic Violence: Treatment Alternatives for the Male Batterer." Unpublished paper, Group Health Cooperative Medical Center, Seattle, WA, 1978.

Busch, Ken, "New Roles for Men and Their Groups in the Battered Women's Movement." Paper presented at the Visions Forum of the Pennsylvania Coalition Against Domestic Violence, Pottstown, PA,October, 1982.

Cantoni, Lucile, "Clinical Issues in Domestic Violence." *Social Casework*. 62:1:3-12, 1981.

Carlson, Bonnie, "Battered Women and Their Assistants." *Social Casework*. 22:6 (November):455-465, 1977.

Carlson, Michelle, "What's Behind Wife Beating." In Shapiro and Shapiro (ed.), *The Women Say/The Men Say*. New York: Dell Publishers, 1979.

Carr, John, "Treating Family Abuse Using a Police Crisis Team Approach." In Roy (eds.), *The Abusive Partner*. New York: Van Nostrand Reinhold, 1982.

Cazenave, Noel, and Murray Straus, "Race, Class, Network Embeddedness and Family Violence: A Search for Potent Support Systems." *Journal of Comparative Family Studies*, in press.

Chodorow, Nancy, *The Reproduction of Mothering: Psychoanalysis and The Sociology of Gender*. Berkeley, CA: University of California Press, 1978.

Cobb, Jonathan, and Richard Sennett, *The Hidden Injuries of Class*. New York: Random, 1973.

Coleman, Karen Howes, "Conjugal Violence: What 33 Men Report." *Journal of Marriage and Family Counseling*. (April):207-213, 1980.

Cornell, Elaine Pedrick, and Richard Gelles, "Adolescent to Parent Violence." *The Urban and Social Change Review*. 15 (Winter):8-14, 1982.

Crites, John, and Louise Fitzgerald, "The Competent Male." *The Counseling Psychologist*. 7:4:10-14, 1978.

David, Deborah, and Robert Brannon (eds.), *The Forty-Nine Percent Majority: The Male Sex Role, 2nd ed.* Reading, MA: Addison-Wesley, 1982.

Davidson, Terry, *Conjugal Crime: Understanding and Changing the Wifebeating Problem*. New York: Hawthorn, 1978.

Davis, Angela, *Women, Race and Class*. New York: Vintage Books, 1981.

Dinnerstein, Dorothy, *The Mermaid and the Minotaur: Sexual Arrangements and the Human Malaise*. New York: Harper and Row, 1976.

Dobash, Emerson R., and Russell Dobash, *Violence Against Wives: A Case Against the Patriarchy*. New York: The Free Press, 1979.

Dobash, Rebecca and Russell Dobash, "Social Science and Social Action: The Case of Wife Beating." *Journal of Family Issues*. (December), 1981.

Dobash, R.E., and R.P. Dobash, "Wife Beating—Still a Common Form of Violence." *Social Work Today*. 9:14-18, 1977.

Dreas, G., D. Ignatov, and T. Brennan, "The Male Batterer: A Model Treatment Program for the Courts." *Federal Probation* 46:4 (December):50-55, 1982.

Dutton, Donald, "An Ecological Nested Theory of Male Violence Toward Intimates." In Caplan (ed.), *Feminist Psychology in Transition*. Montreal: Eden Press, 1984.

Dutton, D., B. Fehr, and H. McEwen, "Severe Wife Battering As Deindividuated Violence." *Victimology*. 7:13-23, 1982.

Dutton, Donald, and Susan Painter, "Traumatic Bonding: The Development of Emotional Attachments in Battered Women and Other Relationships of Intermittent Abuse." *Victimology*. 6:139-155, 1981.

Ehrenreich, Barbara, *The Hearts of Men: American Dreams and the Flight From Commitment*. Garden City, NY: Anchor/Doubleday, 1983.

Etheredge, Lloyd, *A World of Men: Masculinity in U.S. Foreign Policy*. Cambridge, MA: MIT Press, 1978.

Fagan, J., D. Stewart, and K. Hansen, "Violent Men or Violent Husbands? Background Factors and Situational Correlates." In Finkelhor et al. (eds.), *The Dark Side of Families*. Beverly Hills, CA: Sage, 1983.

Farrell, Warren, *The Liberated Man*. New York: Random House, 1974.

Fasteau, Marc Feigen, *The Male Machine*. New York: Delta, 1974.

Faulk, M., "Men Who Assault Their Wives." *Medicine, Science, and Law.* 14:180-183, 1974.

Fein, Robert, "Examining the Nature of Masculinity." In Sarget (ed.), *Beyond Sex Roles*. St. Paul, MN: West Publishing, 1977.

Finkelhor, David, "Common Features of Family Abuse." In Finkelhor et al. (eds.), *The Dark Side of Families*. Beverly Hills, CA: Sage, 1983.

Finkelhor, D., R. Gelles, G. Hotaling, and M. Straus (eds.), *The Dark Side of Families: Current Family Violence Research*. Beverly Hills, CA: Sage, 1983.

Finkelhor, David, and Kersti Yllo, "Forced Sex in Marriage: A Preliminary Research Report." *Crime and Delinquency.* 28:3:459-478, 1982.

Fitch, Frances, and A. Papantonio, "Men Who Batter: Some Pertinent Characteristics." *Journal of Nervous and Mental Disease.* 171:3:190-192, 1983.

Flanzer, Jerry, "Alcohol and Family Violence: Double Trouble." In Roy (ed.), *The Abusive Partner*. New York: Van Nostrand Reinhold, 1982.

Fleming, Jennifer Baker, *Stopping Wife Abuse*. Garden City, NY: Anchor Books, 1979.

Flynn, John, "Recent Findings Related to Wife Abuse." *Social Casework.* 58:1 (January):13-20, 1977.

France, Laureen, "Men Against Violence Against Women." *Aegis: Magazine on Ending Violence Against Women.* (Winter/Spring):37, 1980.

Frank: A Vietnam Veteran. (Transcript) Boston: WGBH Educational Foundation, 1981.

Frank, Phyllis, and Beverly Houghton, *Confronting The Batterer: A Guide to Creating the Spouse Abuse Educational Workshop*. New York: Volunteer Counseling Service of Rockland County, 1982.

Friedan, Betty, *The Second Stage*. New York: Summit Books, 1981.

Ganley, Anne, *Court Mandated Counseling for Men Who Batter* (Trainer's Guide). Washington, DC: Center for Women Policy Studies, 1981.

Garbarino, James, and Gwen Gilliam, *Understanding Abusive Families*. Lexington, MA: Lexington Books, 1980.

Garnet, Shelley, and Doris Moss, "How to Set Up a Counseling Program for Self-Referral Batterers: The AWAIC Model." In Roy (ed.), *The Abusive Partner*. New York: Van Nostrand Reinhold, 1982.

Gayford, John. "The Plight of the Battered Wife." *International Journal of Environmental Studies*. 19:4:283-286, 1977.

Gayford, John, "Battered Wives." *Medical Science and the Law*. 15:237-245, 1975.

Gaylin, William, *Feelings*. New York: Ballantine, 1980.

Geen, Russell, "Effects of Frustration, Attack and Peer Training on Aggressiveness Upon Aggressive Behavior." *Journal of Personality and Social Psychology*. 9:4:316-321, 1968.

Geller, Janet, "Cojoint Therapy: Staff Training and Treatment of the Abuser and the Abused." In Roy (ed.), *The Abusive Partner*. New York: Van Nostrand Reinhold, 1982.

Gelles, Richard, "An Exchange/Social Control Theory." In Finkelhor et al. (eds.), *The Dark Side of Families*. Beverly Hills, CA: Sage, 1983.

Gelles, Richard, "Applying Research on Family Violence to Clinical Practice." *Journal of Marriage and the Family*. 44:1 (February):9-19, 1982.

Gelles, Richard, "Violence in the Family: A Review of Research in the 70's." *Journal of Marriage and the Family*. 42:4:873-885, 1980.

Gelles, Richard, "Methods for Studying Sensitive Family Topics." *American Journal of Orthopsychiatry*. 48:3 (July):408-424, 1978.

Gelles, Richard, "No Place To Go: The Social Dynamics of Marital Violence." In Roy (ed.), *Battered Women*. New York: Van Nostrand Reinhold, 1977.

Gelles, Richard, "Power, Sex, and Violence: The Case of Marital Rape." *Family Coordinator*. 26:4:339-347, 1977.

Gelles, Richard, "Violence and Pregnancy: A Note on the Extent of the Problem and Needed Services." *Family Coordinator*. 24:1 (January), 1975.

Gelles, Richard, "Abused Women: Why Do They Stay?" *Journal of Marriage and the Family*. 38:3:659-668, 1976.

Gelles, Richard, *The Violent Home: A Study of Physical Aggression Between Husbands and Wives*. Beverly Hills, CA: Sage, 1974.

Gerzon, Mark, *A Choice of Heroes: The Changing Faces of American Manhood*. New York: Houghton Mifflin, 1982.

Giles-Sims, Jean, *Wife Battering: A Systems Theory Approach*. New York: Guilford Press, 1983.

Gilligan, Carol, *In a Different Voice: Psychological Theory and Women's Development*. Cambridge, MA: Harvard University Press, 1982.

Goldberg, Herb, *The New Male-Female Relationship*. New York: Signet, 1983.

Goldberg, Herb, *The New Male: From Self-Destruction to Self Care*. New York: Morrow, 1979.

Goldberg, Herb, *The Hazards of Being Male*. New York: Nash, 1976.

Gondolf, Edward, "Men Who Batter: How To Stop Abusing Their Wives." Paper presented at the Family Violence Researchers Conference, University of New Hampshire, August, 1984.

Gondolf, Edward, "Fighting for Control: A Clinical Assessment of Men Who Batter." *Social Casework* (in press).

Gondolf, Edward, "Why Men Batter Women: Male Socialization as the Theoretical Missing Link." *Victimology* (under review).

Goode, William, "Force and Violence in the Family." *Journal of Marriage and the Family*. 33:4 (November):624-636, 1971.

Goodstein, Richard, and Ann Page, "Battered Wife Syndrome: Overview of Dynamics and Treatment." *American Journal of Psychiatry*. 138:8:1036-1043, 1981.

Gottlieb, Benjamin, "Social Networks and Social Support in Community Mental Health." In Gottlieb (ed.), *Social Networks and Social Support*. Beverly Hills, CA: Sage, 1981.

Griffin, Susan, *Women and Nature: The Roaring Inside Her*. New York, NY: Harper and Row, 1980.

Griffin, Susan, *Rape: The Power of Consciousness*. New York: Harper and Row, 1979.

Groth, Nicholas A., *Men Who Rape: The Psychology of the Offender*. New York: Plenam Press, 1979.

Harrison, J., "Warning: The Male Sex Role May Be Hazardous to Your Health." *Journal of Social Issues*. 34:65-86, 1978.

Hartley, Ruth, "Sex Role Pressures and the Socialization of the Male Child." In Joseph Pleck and Jack Sawyer (eds.), *Men and Masculinity*. Englewood Cliffs, NJ: Prentice Hall, 1974.

Haynie, R. L., "Deprivation of Body Pleasure: Origin of Violent Behavior (A Survey of the Literature)." *Child Welfare*. 5:277-297, 1980.

Henslin, James, "On Becoming Male: Reflections of a Sociologist on Childhood and Early Socialization." In James Henslin (ed.), *Down to Earth Sociology, 3rd ed.* New York: Free Press, 1981.

Heppner, M. J., "Counseling the Battered Wife: Myths, Facts, and Decisions." *Personnel and Guidance Journal.* (May):522-525, 1978.

Heppner, Paul, "Counseling Men in Groups." *Personnel and Guidance Journal.* 60:4 (December):249-252, 1981.

Hilberman, Elaine, "Response of Hilberman (to Murray Straus)." In U.S. Community on Civil Rights, *Battered Women: Issues of Public Policy* (A Consultation), Washington, DC, 1981.

Holleb, Gordon, and Walter Abrams, *Alternatives in Community Mental Health: Why Alternative Counseling Centers Started, How They've Fared, Their Future Role.* Boston, MA: Beacon Press, 1975.

Holliday, Laurel, *The Violent Sex: Male Psychobiology and the Evolution of Consciousness.* Guerneville, CA: Bluestocking Books, 1978.

Holmes, Sally Ann, "A Holistic Approach to the Treatment of Violent Families." *Social Casework.* 62 (December):594-600, 1981.

Hooks, Bell, *Ain't I A Woman: Black Women and Feminism.* Boston: South End Press, 1981.

Horney, Karen, "The Dread of Women." *International Journal of Psychoanalysis.* 13:138-360, 1932.

Interrante, Joe, "Dancing Along the Precipice: The Men's Movement in the 80's." *Radical America.* 15:6:53-71, 1981.

Jamus, S., B. Bess, and C. Saltus, *A Sexual Profile of Men in Power.* New York: Warner Books, 1977.

Julty, Sam, *Men's Bodies, Men's Selves.* New York: Delta, 1983.

Kalmuss, Debra, and Murray Straus, "Wife's Marital Dependency and Wife Abuse." *Journal of Marriage and the Family.* 44:2:277-286, 1982.

Kaplan, Stephen, and Eugenie Wheeler, "Survival Skills for Working With Potentially Violent Clients." *Social Casework.* 64:6 (June):339-346, 1983.

Kiley, Dan, *The Peter Pan Principle: Men Who Have Never Grown Up.* New York: Dodd Mead, 1983.

Komarovsky, Mirra, *Dilemmas of Masculinity: A Study of College Youth.* New York: Norton, 1975.

Komisar, Lucy, "Violence and the Masculine Mystique." In D. David and R. Brannon (eds.), *The Forty-Nine Percent Marjority: The Male Sex Role*. Redding, MA: Addison-Wesley, 1976.

Kleckner, James, "Wife Beaters and Beaten Wives: Co-Conspirators in Crimes of Violence." *Psychology*. 15 (February):54-56, 1978.

Langley, Roger, and Richard Levey, *Wife Beating: The Silent Crisis*. New York: Pocket Books, 1977.

Leghorn, Lisa, and Katherine Parker, *Women's Worth: Sexual Economics and the World of Women*. Boston: Routledge and Keagan Paul, 1981.

Lesse, Stanley, "The Status of Violence Against Women: Past, Present, and Future Factors." *American Journal of Psychotherapy*. 33 (April):190-200, 1979.

Levine, Montague, "Interpersonal Violence and Its Effects on the Children: A Study of 50 Families in General Practice." *Medicine, Science and Law*. 15:2:172-175, 1975.

Lewis, Robert (ed.), *Men in Difficult Times*. Englewood Cliffs, NJ: Prentice-Hall, 1981.

Lieberman, Mendel, and Marion Hardie, *Resolving Family and Other Conflicts: Everybody Wins*. Santa Cruz, CA: Unity Press, 1982.

Lion, Joh, "Clinical Aspects of Wifebeating." in Roy (ed.), *Battered Women*. New York: Van Nostrand Reinhold, 1977.

Litewka, Jack, "The Socialized Penis." In Evelyn and Barry Shapiro (eds.), *The Women Say/The Men Say*. New York: Dell Publishing, 1979.

Lloyd, S., R. Cate, and J. Conger, "Family Violence and Service Providers: Implications for Training." *Social Casework*. 64:9 (September):431-435, 1983.

Lyon, Hal, *Tenderness Is Strength: From Machismo to Manhood*. New York: Harper and Row, 1978.

Martin, Del, *Battered Wives*. New York: Pocket Books, 1976.

Matsakis-Scarato, A., "Spouse Abuse Treatment: An Overview." *Aegis*. (Winter/Spring):39-48, 1980.

Meinecke, Christine, "Socialized To Die Younger? Hypermasculinity and Men's Health." *Personnel and Guidance Journal*. 60:4 (December):241-245, 1981.

Mettger, Zak, "Help for Men Who Batter: An Overview of Issues and Programs." *Response.* 5:6 (November/December):1,2,7,8,23, 1982.

Metzger, Mary, "A Social History of Battered Women." *Heresies.* 6:58-68, 1978.

Monahan, John, *Predicting Violent Behavior: An Assessment of Clinical Techniques.* Beverly, CA: Sage, 1981.

Moraga, Cherrie, and Gloria Anzaldua (eds.), *This Bridge Called My Back: Writings by Radical Women of Color.* Watertown, MA: Persephone Press, 1981.

Morrison, Eleanor, and Mila Underhill Price, *Values in Sexuality: A New Approach to Sex Education.* New York: Hart Publishers, 1974.

Morrison, Mary, "Seem Angry? I Am Angry." *Aegis.* 36(Autumn):17-25, 1982.

McClelland, David, *Power: The Inner Experience.* New York: Halsted Press, 1976.

McLaughlin, Laurie, "Children and Women First." A paper presented at the Visions Forum of Pennsylvania Coalition Against Domestic Violence. Pottstown, PA, October, 1982.

Navaco, Raymond, *Anger Control.* Lexington, MA: Lexington Books, 1975.

Nichols, Beverly, B., "The Abused Wife Problem." *Social Casework.* January:27-32, 1976.

Nichols, Jack, *Men's Liberation: A New Definition of Masculinity.* New York: Penguin, 1974.

NSPCC School of Social Work. "Yo Yo Children: A Study of 23 Violent Matrimonial Cases." In Roy (ed.), *Battered Women.* New York: Van Nostrand Reinhold, 1977.

O'Brian, John, "Violence in Divorce Prone Families." *Journal of Marriage and the Family.* 33 (November):692-698, 1971.

O'Neal, James, "Patterns of Gender Role Conflict and Strain: Sexism and Fear of Feminity in Men's Lives." *Personnel and Guidance Journal.* 60:4 (December):203-210, 1981.

Owens, David, and Murray Straus, "Social Structure of Violence in Childhood and Approval of Violence as an Adult." *Aggressive Behavior Journal.* 1:193-211, 1975.

Pagelow, Mildred Daley, *Women-Battering: Victims and Their Experiences.* Beverly Hills, CA: Sage, 1981.

Pelton, Leroy H., "Child Abuse and Neglect: The Myth of Classlessness." *American Journal of Orthopsychiatry.* 48:608-617, 1978.

Peterson, Roger, "Social Class, Social Learning and Wife Abuse." *Social Service Review.* 54:3:390-405, 1980.

Pfouts, J. H., J. H. Schapler, and H. C. Henly, "Forgotten Victims of Family Violence." *Social Work.* 27:4:367-368, 1982.

Pfouts, Jane H., and Connie Renz, "The Future of Wife Abuse Problems." *Social Work.* 26:6:451-455, 1981.

Pinderhughes, Elaine, "Empowerment for Our Clients and for Ourselves." *Social Casework.* 64:6 (June):331-339, 1983.

Piven, Frances Fox, and Richard Cloward, *Poor People's Movements: Why They Succeed, How They Fail.* New York: Random House, 1977.

Pleck, Joseph, *The Myth of Masculinity.* Cambridge, MA: MIT Press, 1981a.

Pleck, Joseph, "Prisoners of Manliness." *Psychology Today.* (September):69-83, 1981b.

Pleck, Joseph, and Jack Sawyer (eds.), *Men and Masculinity.* New York: Prentice-Hall, 1974.

Pleck, E., J. Pleck, M. Grossman, and P. Bart, "The Battered Data Syndrome: A Reply to Steinmentz." *Victimology.* 2:3-4:680-683, 1978.

Powers, Robert, and Irwin Kutash, "Alcohol, Drugs, and Partner Abuse." In Roy (ed.), *The Abusive Partner.* New York: Van Nostrand Reinhold, 1982.

Prescott, James, "Body Pleasure and the Origins of Violence." *Bulletin of the Atomic Scientists.* (November):10-20, 1975.

Quarm, Daisy, and Martin Schwartz, "Legal Reform and the Criminal Court: The Case of Domestic Violence." Unpublished paper. University of Cincinnati, Cincinnati, OH, 1983.

Raiha, Nancy, "Spouse Abuse in the Military Community: Factors Influencing Incidence and Treatment." In Roy (ed.), *The Abusive Partner.* New York: Van Nostrand Reinhold, 1982.

RAVEN, "A Presentation of the RAVEN Project Goals and Objectives." Unpublished proposal. RAVEN, St. Louis, MO, 1981.

Roberts, Albert, "A National Survey of Services for Batterers." In Roy (ed.), *The Abusive Partner.* New York: Van Nostrand Reinhold, 1982.

Roberts, Albert (ed.), *Battered Women and Their Families: Intervention Strategies and Treatment Programs*. New York: Springer, 1984.

Rosen, Gerald, *The Relaxation Book: An Illustrated Self-Help Program*. New York: Prentice-Hall, 1977.

Rosenbaum, Alan, and K. Daniel O'Leary, "Children: The Unintended Victims of Marital Violence." *American Journal of Orthopsychiatry*. 51:4 (October):692-699, 1982.

Rossi, Alice, "Transition to Parenthood." *Journal of Marriage and the Family*. 30:1:26-39, 1968.

Roy, Maria, "Four Thousand Partners in Violence: A Trend Analysis." In Roy (ed.), *The Abusive Partner*. New York: Van Nostrand Reinhold, 1982a.

Roy, Maria, "The Nature of Abusive Behavior." In Roy (ed.), *The Abusive Partner*. New York: Van Nostrand Reinhold, 1982b.

Roy, Maria, "Current Survey of 150 Cases." In Roy (ed.), *Battered Women*. New York: Van Nostrand Reinhold, 1977.

Roy, Maria, (ed.) *The Abusive Partner: An Analysis of Domestic Battering*. New York: Van Nostrand Reinhold, 1982.

Roy, Maria, (ed.) *Battered Women: A Psychosociological Study of Domestic Violence*. New York: Van Nostrand Reinhold, 1977.

Rubin, Lillian, *Intimate Strangers: Men and Women Together*. New York: Harper and Row, 1983.

Rubin, Lillian, "The Marriage Bed." In Shapiro and Shapiro (ed.), *The Women Say/The Men Say*. New York: Dell, 1979.

Rubin, Lillian, *Worlds of Pain: Life in the Working Class Family*. New York: Basic, 1976.

Russell, Diana E. H., *Rape in Marriage*. New York: MacMillan Publishers, 1982.

Ryan, Regina Sara, and John Travis, *Wellness Workbook*. Berkeley, CA: Ten Speed Press, 1980.

Saunders, Daniel G., "Marital Violence: Dimension of the Problem and Modes of Intervention." *Journal of Marriage and Family Counseling*. 3:1:43-52, 1977.

Sanford, John, *The Invisible Partners: How The Male and Female in Each of Us Affects Our Relationships*. New York: Paulist Press, 1980.

Sattel, Jack, "The Inexpressive Male: Tragedy or Sexual Politics." *Social Problems*. 28 (April):469-477, 1976.

Schechter, Susan, *Women and Male Violence: The Visions and Struggles of the Battered Women's Movement.* Boston: South, 1982.

Scher, Murray, "Men in Hiding: A Challenge for the Counselor." *The Personnel and Guidance Journal.* 60:4 (December):199-203, 1981.

Schultz, Leroy G., "The Wife Assaulter." *Corrective Psychiatry and Journal of Social Therapy.* 6 (February):103-111, 1960.

Schumm, W. R., M. J. Martin, S. R. Bolman, and A. P. Jurich, "Classifying Family Violence: Wither the Woozle." *Journal of Family Issues.* 3:3:319-340, 1982.

Schuyler, Marcella, "Battered Wives: An Emerging Sexual Problem." *Social Work.* 21 (November):488-491, 1976.

Selye, Hans, *Stress Without Distress.* New York: Signet, 1975.

Sexton, Patricia, *The Feminized Male: Classrooms, White Collar, and The Decline of Manliness.* New York: Vintage Books, 1973.

Shainess, Natalie, "Vulnerability to Violence: Masochism as a Process." *American Journal of Psychotherapy.* 33 (April):174-189, 1979.

Shainess, Natalie, "Psychological Aspects of Wife Battering." In Roy (ed.), *Battered Women.* New York: Van Nostrand Reinhold, 1977.

Shapiro, Evelyn, and Barry Shapiro (eds.), *The Women Say/The Men Say: The Women's Liberation Movement and Men's Consciousness.* New York: Delta, 1979.

Shepard, Herbert, "Men in Organizations: Some Reflections." In Sargent (ed.), *Beyond Sex Roles.* St. Paul, MN: West Publishing Company, 1977.

Singer, June, *Androgyny: Toward a New Theory of Sexuality.* Garden City, NY: Anchor Books, 1977.

Snell, J., R. Rosenwald, and A. Rokey, "The Wifebeaters Wife." *Archives of General Psychiatry.* 11:109-114, 1964.

Snodgrass, Jon (ed.), *For Men Against Sexism.* New York: Times Change Press, 1977.

Stacey, William, and Anson Shupe, *The Family Secret: Domestic Violence in America.* Boston: Beacon, 1983.

Star, Barbara, *Helping the Abuser: Intervening Effectively in Family Violence.* New York: Family Service Assoc. of America, 1983.

Star, Barbara, "Reducing Family Violence." *The Urban and Social Change Review.* 15 (Winter): 15-20, 1982.

Star, Barbara, "Patterns in Family Violence." *Social Casework.* 61:6:334-346, 1980.

Stark, E., A. Flitcraft, and W. Frazier, "Medicine and Patriarchal Violence: The Social Construction of a 'Private' Event." *International Journal of Health Services.* 9:3:461-494, 1979.

Steinmetz, Suzanne, "Women and Violence: Victims and Perpetrators." *American Journal of Psychotherapy.* 34 (July):334-349, 1980.

Steinmetz, Suzanne, "Wifebeating, Husbandbeating: A Comparison of the Use of Physical Violence Between Spouses to Resolve Marital Fights." In Roy (ed.), *Battered Women.* New York: Van Nostrand Reinhold, 1977.

Stodder, James, "Confessions of a Candy-Ass Roughneck." In Shapiro (eds.), *The Women Say/The Men Say.* New York: Dell Publishing, 1979.

Stone, I. F., "Machismo in Washington." In Pleck and Sawyer (eds.), *Men and Masculinity.* Englewood Cliffs, NJ: Prentice-Hall, 1974.

Straus, Murray, "Victims and Aggressors in Marital Violence." *American Behavioral Scientist.* 23:5 (May/June):681-704, 1980.

Straus, Murray, "A Sociological Perspective on the Prevention and Treatment of Wifebeating." In Roy (ed.), *Battered Women.* New York: Van Nostrand Reinhold, 1977.

Straus, Murray, "Leveling, Civility, and Violence in the Family." *Journal of Marriage and the Family.* 36 (February):13-29, 1974.

Straus, M., R. Gelles, and S. Steinmets, *Behind Closed Doors: Violence in the American Family.* New York: Anchor/Doubleday, 1980.

Sullivan, Gail, "Cooperation of Alternative Services: The Battered Women's Movement as a Case Study." *Catalyst: A Socialist Journal of the Social Services.* 14:39-58, 1982.

Tavris, Carol, *Anger: The Misunderstood Emotion.* New York: Simon and Schuster, 1983.

Tavris, Carol, and Carole Offir, *The Longest War: Sex Differences in Perspective.* New York: Harcourt Brace Jovanovich, 1977.

Tidmarsh, Mannes, "Violence in Marriage: The Relevance of Structural Factors." *Social Work Today.* 7:2 (April):36-48, 1976.

Tiger, Lionel, *Men in Groups.* New York: Random House, 1964.

Toch, Hans, *Violent Men: An Inquiry into the Psychology of Violence.* Chicago: Aldine Publishers, 1969.

U.S. Commission on Civil Rights, *Battered Women: Issues of Public Policy.* A consultation sponsored by the U.S. Commission of Civil Rights, Washington, D.C. (January 30-31), 1978.

Van Vuuren, Nancy. *The Subversion of Women.* Philadelphia: Westminster Press, 1973.

Walker, Lenore, "The Battered Woman Syndrome Study." In Finkelhor et al. (eds.), *The Dark Side of Families.* Beverly Hills, CA: Sage, 1983.

Walker, Lenore, *The Battered Women.* New York: Harper, 1979.

Wallace, Michelle, *Black Macho and the Myth of Superwoman.* New York: Dial Press, 1978.

Wardell, L., D. Gillespie, and A. Leffler, "Science and Violence Against Wives." In Finkelhor et al. (eds.), *The Dark Side of Families.* Beverly Hills, CA: Sage, 1983.

Warren, Donald, *Helping Networks: How People Cope With Problems in the Urban Community.* Notre Dame, IN: University of Notre Dame Press, 1981.

Watson, C., A. Rosenberg, and N. Petrik, "Incidence of Wife-Battering in Male Psychiatric Hospital Patients: Are Special Treatment Programs Needed?" *Psychological Reports.* 51:2:536-566, 1982.

Watts, Deborah, and Christine Courtois, "Trends in the Treatment of Men Who Commit Violence Against Women." *Personnel and Guidance Journal.* 60:4 (December):244-249, 1981.

Weitzman, Jack, and Karen Dreen, "Wife Beating: A View of the Marital Dyad." *Social Casework.* 63 (May):259-265, 1982.

Yllo, Kersti, and Murray Straus, "Interpersonal Violence Among Married and Cohabiting Couples." Paper read at the annual meeting of the National Council on Family Relations, 1978.

Zibergeld, Bernard, *The Shrinking of America.* Boston: Little Brown, 1983.

Zibergeld, Bernard, *Male Sexuality: A Guide to Sexual Fulfillment.* Boston: Little Brown, 1978.

Index